UNMASKING F
AND ATTACH ...THE
PSYCHOANALYTIC SPACE

What do we see? What do we think?
What do we feel?

The Centre for Attachment-Based Psychoanalytic Psychotherapy

UNMASKING RACE, CULTURE, AND ATTACHMENT IN THE PSYCHOANALYTIC SPACE

What do we see? What do we think? What do we feel?

THE JOHN BOWLBY MEMORIAL CONFERENCE MONOGRAPH 2005

Edited by

Kate White

KARNAC

LONDON   NEW YORK

Published in 2006 by
H. Karnac (Books) Ltd.
6 Pembroke Buildings, London NW10 6RE
on behalf of
The Centre for Attachment-Based Psychoanalytic Psychotherapy

British Library Cataloguing in Publication Data

A C.I.P. for this book is available from the British Library

ISBN: 1-85575-405-3

Typeset by RefineCatch Ltd, Bungay, Suffolk

Printed in the United Kingdom by
Biddles Ltd, King's Lynn (www.biddles.co.uk)

www.karnacbooks.com

CONTENTS

CONTRIBUTORS

Barbara Ashton is a member of the Centre for Attachment-based Psychoanalytic Psychotherapy (CAPP). In the past year she has been the chair of the referrals committee at CAPP. She has a private practice in North London and for the past seven years has been involved as a psychotherapist with Immigrant Counselling and Psychotherapy (ICAP), a voluntary organization based in Finsbury Park, North London. ICAP was set up primarily to address the needs of the Irish community in the London area, but has an open referral policy providing low cost services to a wide variety of people.

Farhad Dalal is a supervisor and training group analyst at the Institute of Group Analysis, London. He is an Associate Fellow at the University of Hertfordshire's Business School, in the Complexity and Management Centre. He works in private practice as a psychotherapist and supervisor, and also works with organizations. His publications include the books *Taking the Group Seriously* (1998, Jessica Kingsley), and *Race, Colour and the Processes of Racialization: New Perspectives from Group Analysis, Psychoanalysis and Sociology* (2002, Brunner-Routledge).

Cascia Davis is a member of the Centre for Attachment-based Psychoanalytic Psychotherapy. She has a private practice in South London in addition to working at a G.P. surgery. Cascia is a social worker and has worked for many years in the field of adoption and fostering. She works part time in a voluntary agency providing counselling and support to adopted adults. She also provides intermediary support to assist them to search for their birth family and to reunite.

Zack Eleftheriadou is a Chartered Counselling Psychologist and Psychotherapist. She works as a psychotherapist in private practice in North London. She has worked as a clinician at the Medical Foundation for the Care of Victims of Torture, working with young refugees, and at Nafsiyat Inter-cultural Therapy Centre. She is a lecturer and trainer in cross-cultural psychology, psychotherapy and child development. She has published widely, including the book *Transcultural Counselling*. She is the ex-Chair of the British Association of Counselling Division "Race and Cultural Education in Counselling" (RACE).

Bernice Laschinger had many years of experience in community mental health prior to becoming an attachment-based psychoanalytic psychotherapist. She is a member of CAPP where she is a training therapist, teacher and supervisor and has been very involved in the development of CAPP's training curriculum, particularly with the integration of the relational model of psychoanalysis into the course.

Kimberlyn Leary is the Director of Psychology and Psychology Training at the Cambridge Health Alliance and a Visiting Associate Professor at Harvard Medical School. A graduate of the Michigan Psychoanalytic Institute, she is also a Faculty Affiliate at the Program on Negotiation at Harvard Law School where she is engaged in interdisciplinary inquiry on relational processes in negotiation and in clinical practice. Her published work addresses postmodern and relational perspectives in teaching, supervision and psychotherapy and racial and cultural issues in clinical settings. Her 1997 paper on race and self-disclosure won the American Psychoanalytic Association's Karl Menninger Prize. She has an active clinical practice in psychotherapy and psychoanalysis.

Irris Singer is a training therapist, writes, supervises and teaches at CAPP. Born into an immigrant family with mixed race Jewish parents, Irris spent the Second World War years in a very English village, and became aware of difference early in her life. She spent her formative years in Israel within the idealised concept of "A Land of Difference". Understanding the very nature of that social and individual difference became central to Irris's clinical and theoretical work and led to her co-founding the Counselling Centre for Women, Israel in 1985. Where possible she transfers what she learns in the clinical and teaching space back into the social and political arena, where she is active in Israel/Palestine peace politics.

Kate White is a training therapist, supervisor and teacher at the Centre for Attachment-based Psychoanalytic Psychotherapy. Formerly senior lecturer at South Bank University in the Department of Nursing and Community Health Studies, she has used her extensive experience in adult education to contribute to the innovative psychotherapy curriculum developed at CAPP. In addition to working as an individual psychotherapist, Kate runs workshops on the themes of attachment and trauma in clinical practice. Informed by her experience of growing up in South Africa, she has long been interested in the impact of race and culture on theory and on clinical practice.

ACKNOWLEDGEMENTS

Thanks to the Bowlby Memorial Conference 2005 Planning Group: Sarah Benamer, Christine Blake, Richard Bowlby, Stephanie Davis, Maeja Raicar and Judy Yellin for their creative work in producing a stimulating and groundbreaking conference which has enabled the emergence of this exciting and timely monograph. Also, I give a special thank you to all the contributors to the conference whose innovative work can now reach a much wider audience.

Thanks to our 12th John Bowlby Memorial Lecturer 2005, Kimberlyn Leary, for her inspiring presentation around which this conference was planned.

Special thanks to Sybille Berger for the generous donation of her painting for the cover of this book. It was chosen especially to reflect the complexity of the themes explored in this monograph.

Finally thanks to Oliver Rathbone for his continuing belief in the value of publishing these monographs and to Leena Hakkinen and Catherine Foley at Karnac Books for their patience and support.

Kate White
November 2005

Introduction to the monograph of the 12th John Bowlby Memorial Conference 2005

Kate White

This collection of papers addresses the often hidden and ignored subject of the relationship between attachment, race and culture. There is a significant gap in the development of attachment theory, and that is the issue of racism and its impact on the lives of individuals and communities. Since people and their sense of self develops within differing cultural contexts and inequalities of power relations (Park, 2004, p. 134), the complex constellation of power dynamics, as lived out in people's lives, is a major factor to be considered in any account of our psychological development.

Bernice Laschinger reminds us that, despite this gap, attachment theorists have frequently engaged with the impact of culture and have undertaken cross-cultural research studies. She goes on to say that:

> There is a penetrating "moral and social vision" which runs through Bowlby's work. Core to his work was the overriding force of the social world on the structuring of relationship. His early work (Bowlby, 1952) reflected his passionate concern with the "impact of war, social disruption and emotional poverty" on the rights of children to love and care. In recent centuries, however, racism, in its underpinning of power inequality in relationships, has been primary in the distortion, denial and destruction of attachment bonds. This implies that no proper understanding of relationships can avoid engagement with the issues of racism unless one is determined to disregard questions of power. [Laschinger, 2006, p. 5]

1

With this challenge, the collection of papers in this volume is a contribution to furthering our discussion and understanding of these important questions, particularly as they emerge in the therapeutic relationship.

In our planning of the conference we argued that too often issues of race, culture and ethnicity are seen as relevant only to black and ethnic minority psychotherapists and clients. It was felt that all psychotherapists and their clients bring a rich diversity of ethnic and cultural narratives to the clinical encounter. Each of us has a unique and complex sense of who we feel ourselves to be, as well as who others expect us to be, in the ever-shifting contexts of our individual families, societies and cultures. Each of us is likely to grapple with feelings of inclusion and exclusion, belonging and alienation, visibility and invisibility, power and powerlessness.

The conference posed some key questions. How can we as therapists use our own experiences of difference in order to get alongside our clients, without collapsing difference and sameness into each other? Can we hold the tension between them? What is our responsibility as psychotherapists and supervisors for engaging in these issues, both in our own individual development and in the clinical setting, in the context of a society that structures our identities on the basis of colour coded racial categories?

Over the conference weekend we had the opportunity to discuss the implications of the development of our identities within attachment relationships which are themselves embedded in particular constellations of racial and ethnic power dynamics. The speakers invited us to think about how we can understand the very real impact of categories of identity, such as race, on the formation of our selves, at the same time as recognizing their socially constructed nature. Other questions posed by the contributors were about how these categories help to give us and our clients a secure sense of identity, and conversely how they constrict our sense of our own and our clients' possibilities.

The first paper by Farhad Dalal is an in depth introduction to the complexity of the territory being explored in this monograph. He challenges us to reorient our thinking by asking us to consider four questions. What is racism? How does psychoanalysis explain the phenomenon of racism? How can attachment theory be used to think about racism? Finally, why is it that attachment theory is located outside psychoanalysis by psychoanalysts as much as by attachment theorists? He then goes on to describe his own unique contribution to the field. Having exposed the hollowness of race as a category, he offers his theory of the process of racialization and the accompanying dehumanizing process of "othering" as a much more comprehensive and radical alternative.

Zack Eleftheriadou's chapter revisits the concepts of "race" and "culture" and expands current thinking using research findings from the fields of child psychology and social psychology. She argues that in order to understand cross-cultural relationships, we need to incorporate a psychosocial framework. She concludes with a clinical case study of her work with a child that brings the theoretical discussion to life and provides a vivid illustration of the clinical implications of this approach.

In the next section of the monograph Barbara Ashton, Cascia Davis and Irris Singer, write about their experiences in response to the following challenging questions. Can our individual narratives in relation to race, culture and attachment be unmasked in the therapeutic dyad to reveal our human connectedness? How can the exploration of our own racial and cultural identities provide us with therapeutic tools to work within and across multiple categories of cultural identity?

They each describe their experience in different contexts ranging from psychotherapeutic work with individuals who might be refugees or migrants, to work with bereaved parents' groups in Israel and Palestine. They move from the individual to the wider social and political context and back again as they narrate their personal and professional stories. These accounts provide a rich and interesting picture of the complexity of working across multiple categories of cultural identity in therapeutic relationships and the personal and political issues both within and without.

The Bowlby Memorial Lecture 2005 was given by Kimberlyn Leary. Her paper entitled "How race is lived in the consulting room", set in the context of the United States post-9/11, is a rich and inspiring account of her work with William and how the racialized subjectivities of therapist and client emerged in their therapeutic relationship. She challenges us to engage more deeply with questions that are difficult to reflect on because they take us to places where power has been brutally exploited and where differences of race have such a traumatic history. Her concept of "racial enact-ment" is explored with several clinical vignettes. Kimberlyn offers an insight into how these may become opportunities for transform-ation if both parties in the encounter can tolerate their exposure to the other.

> The analyst's working subjectivity regarding his or her racial assumptions must be subject to honest and compassionate scrutiny. This requires a willingness to bear a measure of discomfort in order to make it possible to learn with and from patients. [Leary, 2006, p. 87]

It has been a privilege to bring together these papers which I think provide a sustained and deep engagement with this frequently neg-lected subject at a level of complexity not often possible with a theme that is associated with such pain and conflict.

References

Bowlby, J. (1952). *Maternal Care and Mental Health*, 2nd edn, World Health Organization: Monograph Series, No. 2. Geneva: World Health Organization.

Laschinger, B. (2006). Attachment theory and the John Bowlby Memorial Lecture. In: K. White (Ed.), *Unmasking Race, Culture and Attachment. What do we see? What do we think? What do we feel?* pp. 5–9. London: Karnac.

Leary, K. (2006). How race is lived in the consulting room. In: K. White (Ed.), *Unmasking Race, Culture and Attachment. What do we see? What do we think? What do we feel?* pp. 75–89. London: Karnac.

Park, J. (2004). Walking the tightrope: Developing an attachment-based/relational curriculum for trainee psychotherapists. *Attachment and Human Development Journal*, 6: 131–140.

Attachment theory and the John Bowlby Memorial Lecture

A short history

Bernice Laschinger

T he theme of the John Bowlby Memorial Conference 2005 addresses a notable gap in how attachment theory has developed: racism. Its absence from the literature contrasts markedly with the theory's engagement with culture. From its early beginnings in the work of Mary Ainsworth, attachment theory has undertaken cross-cultural research in countries as diverse as Kenya, Israel, Japan and Germany.

There is a penetrating "moral and social vision" which runs through Bowlby's work. Core to his work was the overriding force of the social world on the structuring of relationship. His early work reflected his passionate concern with the impact of "war, social disruption and emotional poverty" on the rights of children to love and care. In recent centuries, however, racism, in its underpinning of power inequality in relationships, has been primary in the distortion, denial and destruction of attachment bonds. This implies that no proper understanding of relationships can avoid engagement with the issues of racism unless one is determined to disregard questions of power.

The themes of this year's conference link with the fundamental values which are articulated in Bowlby's earliest works. His post-war

5

studies of refugee children led to the publication of his seminal work, *Maternal Care and Mental Health* by the World Health Organization in 1952. He also studied children in hospital and a residential nursery, in conjunction with James Robertson who filmed them. The documented sequence of the children's responses to separation in terms of protest, detachment and despair provided evidence of separation anxiety. The impact of these ideas on the development of child care policy has been enormous. The 2001 Bowlby Lecturer, Michael Rutter, discussed institutional care and the role of the state in promoting recovery from neglect and abuse. His lecture was a testament to the continuing relevance of Bowlby's thinking to contemporary social issues

Although Bowlby joined the British Psychoanalytic Society in the 1930s and received his training from Joan Riviere and Melanie Klein, he became increasingly sceptical of their focus on the inner fantasy life of the child rather than real life experience, and tended towards what would now be termed a relational approach. Thus, in searching for a theory which could explain the anger and distress of separated young children, Bowlby turned to disciplines outside psychoanalysis such as ethology. He became convinced of the relevance of animal and particularly primate behaviour to our understanding of the normal process of attachment. These relational concepts presented a serious challenge to the closed world of psychoanalysis in the 1940s, and earned Bowlby the hostility of his erstwhile colleagues for several decades.

The maintenance of physical proximity by a young animal to a preferred adult is found in a number of animal species. This suggested to Bowlby that attachment behaviour has a survival value, the most likely function of which is that of care and protection, particularly from predators. It is activated by conditions such as sickness, fear and fatigue. Threat of loss leads to anxiety and anger; actual loss leads to anger and sorrow. When efforts to restore the bond fail, attachment behaviour may diminish, but will persist at an unconscious level and may become reactivated by reminders of the lost adult, or new experiences of loss.

Attachment theory's basic premise is that, from the beginning of life, the baby human has a primary need to establish an emotional bond with a care-giving adult. Attachment is seen as a source of human motivation as fundamental as are those of food and sex.

Bowlby (1979, p. 129) postulated that

> Attachment behaviour is any form of behaviour that results in a person attaining or maintaining proximity to some other preferred and differentiated individual ... While especially evident during early childhood, attachment behaviour is held to characterize human beings from the cradle to the grave.

Attachment theory highlights the importance of mourning in relation to trauma and loss. An understanding of the relevance of this to therapeutic practice was a vital element in the foundation of the Centre for Attachment-based Psychoanalytic Psychotherapy (CAPP). The consequences of disturbed and unresolved mourning processes was a theme taken up by Colin Murray Parkes when he gave the first John Bowlby Memorial Lecture.

Mary Ainsworth, an American psychologist who became Bowlby's lifelong collaborator, established the inter-connectedness between attachment behaviour, caregiving in the adult, and exploration in the child. While the child's need to explore, and the need for proximity might seem contradictory, they are in fact complementary. It is the mother's provision of a secure base, to which the child can return after exploration, which enables the development of self-reliance and autonomy. Ainsworth developed the "Strange Situation Test" for studying individual differences in the attachment patterns of young children. She was able to correlate these to their mothers' availability and responsiveness. Her work provided both attachment theory and psychoanalysis with empirical support for some basic premises. This provided the necessary link between attachment concepts and their application to individual experience in a clinical setting.

Over the last two decades the perspective of attachment theory has been greatly extended by the work of Mary Main, who was another Bowlby Lecturer. She developed the "Adult Attachment Interview" in order to study the unconscious processes that underlie the behavioural pattern of attachment identified by Mary Ainsworth. Further support came from the perspective of infant observation and developmental psychology developed by yet another Bowlby Lecturer, Daniel Stern. The Bowlby Lecturer for 2000, Allan Schore, presented important developments in the new field of neuropsychoanalysis describing emerging theories of how attachment experiences in early life shape the developing brain.

The links between attachment theory and psychoanalysis have also been developed. Jo Klein, a great supporter of CAPP and also a former contributor to the Bowlby Conference, has explored these links in psychotherapeutic practice. In particular, the 1998 Bowlby Lecturer, Stephen Mitchell, has identified a paradigm shift away from drive theory within psychoanalysis. His proposed "relational matrix" links attachment theory to other relational psychoanalytic theories that find so much resonance in the current social and cultural climate. Within this area of convergence, between attachment research and developmental psychoanalysis, the 1999 Bowlby Lecturer, Peter Fonagy, has developed the concept of "mentalization", extending our understanding of the importance of the reflective function, particularly in adversity.

In similar vein, the work of Beatrice Beebe, the 2001 Bowlby Lecturer, represents another highly creative development in the unfolding relational narrative of the researcher-clinician dialogue. Her unique research has demonstrated how the parent infant interaction creates a distinct system organized by mutual influence and regulation which are reproduced in the adult therapeutic relationship.

In the movement to bring the body into the forefront of relational theory and practice, the 2003 Bowlby Lecturer, Susie Orbach, a CAPP Trustee, has been a leading pioneer. It was the publication of her groundbreaking books, *Fat is a Feminist Issue* and *Hunger Strike*, that introduced a powerful and influential approach to the study of the body in its social context. Over the last decade, one of her major interests has been the construction of sexuality and bodily experience in the therapeutic relationship.

The contribution of last year's Bowlby Lecturer, Jody Messler Davies, to the development of the American Relational model has been seminal. Her integration (with Mary-Gail Frawley) of trauma theory and relational psychoanalysis in the understanding of sexual abuse has had a great impact, (Davies, J. M., & Frawley, M. G. (1994)). Her conceptualization of the transference–countertransference as the vehicle for expressing dissociated traumatic experience was one of the first clinical applications of this relational approach

Within this groundbreaking tradition, this year's John Bowlby

Lecturer, Kimberlyn Leary's work courageously illuminates the impact of racism on the clinical process, (Leary, 2000a, 2000b). She vividly conveys the constriction and shame generated by the collision of two "racialized subjectivities" in the therapeutic relationship. The importance of her contribution lies in her understanding of its transformative potential. Drawing on relational psychoanalysis she shows the possibility for reparation that is opened up when both therapist and client break the silence. It is through the open "scrutiny" of their different "race experience" and "race history" that they can begin to find their sameness.

References

Bowlby, J. (1952). *Maternal Care and Mental Health*, 2nd edn, World Health Organization: Monograph Series, No. 2. Geneva: World Health Organization.

Bowlby, J. (1979). *The Making and Breaking of Affectional Bonds*. London: Tavistock.

Davies, J. M., & Frawley, M. G. (1994). *Treating the Adult Survivor of Childhood Sexual Abuse: A Psychoanalytic Perspective*. New York: Basic Books.

Harris, A. (2000). Haunted talk, healing action. Commentary on paper by Kimberlyn Leary. *Psychoanalytic Dialogues, 10*: 655–662.

Leary, K. (2000a). Race in psychoanalytic space, pp 313–330. In: M. Dimen, & V. Goldner (Eds.), *Gender in Psychoanalytic Space—Between Clinic and Culture*. New York: Other Press.

Leary, K. (2000b). Racial enactments in dynamic treatment. *Psychoanalytic Dialogues, 10*: 639–654.

Racism

Processes of detachment, dehumanization and hatred

Farhad Dalal

A colleague described an experience whilst travelling on a train during a visit to London. She became aware that she was the only white person in the carriage and this made her feel frightened and completely alone. This was a remarkable experience because patently she was not alone; she was in a carriage full of people.

What is going on? How is it that she feels alone when patently she is not? Is this kind of experience "racist"? And if so, why?

I do not stand in judgement of my colleague, because I can recognize myself having such experiences continually. Sometimes these differentiations are innocuous or humorous, at other times critical and deadly. The triggers vary hugely: sometimes colour, at other times beliefs, attitudes, behaviours or something else altogether.

This is a way of saying that in focussing on race and racism, I am not suggesting that this is the primary difference, or the only meaningful difference that needs to be attended to. In fact what I am going to put forward is part of a general theory of difference—in which the fiction called "race" is but one element.

The short vignette speaks to the first of my four questions—just what is racism? My other questions being, how does psychoanalysis tend to explain the phenomenon of racism? Third, how can attachment theory be used to think about racism? And fourth, how and why is it that attachment theory is located outside psychoanalysis by psychoanalysts as much as by attachment theorists? I won't be speaking in a neat linear fashion to each of the questions in turn as the answers to one problematize the others.

What is racism?

Is racism a pathology that only some are afflicted with, or is it endemic to the human condition so that all of us are subject to it? Is it the case, as was said in some circles in the 1970's and even now, that only whites can be racist? And what of the function of racism? Is it something destructive or something useful, an adaptive mechanism that has evolved?

Racism tends to be described in two sorts of ways: The first description is at the level of the social world and says that racism is a form of organizing peoples, commodities and the relationships between them by utilizing a notion of race. The second description begins in the world of emotions and says that racism consists of the feelings of hatred, disgust, repulsion and other negative emotions felt and expressed by one group for another.

Now, in general, psychoanalysis tends to look for the causes of things that take place in the "external" social world in goings on in the "internal" psychological world of individuals. For example:

A group consists of individuals in a relationship to one another; and therefore the understanding of [the individual's] personality is the foundation for the understanding of social life. [Klein, 1959, p. 247]

all sociological problems are ultimately reducible to problems of individual psychology. [Fairbairn, 1935, p. 241]

the basis of group psychology is the psychology of the individual, and especially of the individual's personal integration. [Winnicott, 1965, p. 146]

It follows then that psychoanalysis is bound to look for explanations of racism (that is antipathies between peoples taking place in the social world) in the internal world of individuals. We can see that the question of "what is racism?" cannot be separated from speculations about its causes.

Psychoanalysis offers four different kinds of explanation for adult behaviours in general. The first explanation is akin to transference in the sense that Freud first spoke of it—repeating without remembering. Here, events and behaviours in adult life are said to be repetitions and versions of patterns laid down during infancy and childhood. If these developmental events are repeatedly experienced as traumatic then the adult will behave in disturbed and sometimes aggressive, perhaps racist ways. The second kind of explanation draws on the individual/group dichotomy. What would be said here is that racism is some kind of group phenomenon that sweeps up individuals in its path through the process of contagion or something similar. In this way of thinking good people find themselves behaving badly because of being swept up by the group. In this way of thinking when in groups, individuals loose their civilized sensibilities and revert to some primeval savage state. The third explanation says that we are driven to act in certain ways by our biological and genetic inheritance—specifically the instincts. The fourth explanation, and by far the most common place, features the mechanisms of splitting, repression and projection.

I will begin my critique with the last of these.

Projection

The idea of projection lies at the heart of most psychoanalytic explanations of social phenomena, and proceeds in the following way: difficulties arising in the internal world of an individual (say aggressive impulses) which cannot be managed for whatever reason, are split off from consciousness, repressed and projected into some object or person in the external world. The subject now comes to experience the object/person as difficult in itself (in this instance, aggressive). This theory does work, but in a limited way, at the level of a particular individual. This theory would explain why it is that this or that particular individual has hateful feelings towards blacks or some other group of people. However, it does not explain *how* and *why* it is that a whole group of people should simultaneously come to hold hateful feelings towards certain other groups. There is also the issue of why black people rather than (say) nurses should come to be used as containers for these unwanted and problematic aspects of the self. And why is it in one context black people come to be these receptacles, and in another context Protestants, and so on. One sort of answer that is put forward to these challenges in psychoanalytic writings, is to say that these groupings have previously been "socially sanctioned" as deserving of these projections and so are already denigrated. But this answer actually avoids the central issue that is: how do these groupings come to be socially sanctioned in the first place? It is also the case that this sort of theory does not address what happens to the unwanted aspects of the individuals who constitute these denigrated groups—blacks, Jews, women, for example—where are they to project the problematic aspects of their psyches? Are they not going to be allowed the same privilege as their white counter parts of getting rid of problematic aspects of their internal worlds through the mechanism of splitting and projecting? In sum, what this sort of theory does is to say that the psychological mechanisms of individuals exploit pre-existing social conditions to manage internal psychological difficulties. It does not engage with the problematic of how those social conditions, specifically racism, came to be generated in the first place.

Similarity and difference

Notions of similarity and difference have become buzzwords in this territory. However, in the psychoanalytic literature, the notions of similarity and difference are rendered curiously a-social, as though all differences were equivalent. They are not. A stranger knocking unexpectedly at the door, will elicit quite different associations and emotions depending on whether "the stranger" is a young black man, or a white man in a suit. It will also depend on who is opening the door, and where the door is. In other words one cannot leave context out of the analysis. There is no such thing as "the stranger" in the abstract—strangers are always particular, embodied and situated. Animosity is by no means the "natural" and inevitable response to meeting a difference. The reactions are bound to be predicated on the meanings attributed to, and associated with, that difference. Thus we cannot leave the social context out of the analysis; and if we do leave it out, then it makes the analysis reductive.

The thing is that we are never just "strangers" to each other, we are also simultaneously "familiars". Let me put it this way— between any two individuals there are an infinity of similarities and differences. I am similar to you by virtue of at least one attribute, and *in the same moment* I am different by virtue of at least one other attribute. Thus similarity and differences are not absolutes, and neither are they opposites. The experience of similarity and difference can always be deconstructed. For example, in this moment, do you experience me as similar or different to you? On what basis, race, culture, ethnicity or some other category? If you experience me as similar, why are you inclined in that direction at this moment, and what have you done with the differences? And if you are experiencing me as different, what have you done with the similarities? Why?

These positivist ways of thinking about similarity and difference have become taken for granted and unquestioned in our profession—it would appear that people are *either* similar *or* different to each other. For example Basch-Kahre (1984), takes it for granted that it is a universal truth that one is inevitably afraid of strangers. Her explanation says that the sources of the fear of strangers are to be found early on in the developmental story, when the baby seeks to keep the father out of the picture by making him unknown and therefore a stranger. This repressed memory is said to be reactivated in adult life with the appearance of any strangers, which results in the old hatred towards the father being projected onto contemporary strangers. She says: "This happens when confronted with people and cultures in which we can discover *no similarity with ourselves*" (1984, p. 62; italics added). But clearly this is an impossibility—that there is "no similarity" between analyst and analysand. We have to ask of the analyst a deeper question—how does the analyst manage the extraordinary feat of experiencing "no similarity"? Recall the vignette at the start of the paper.

In sum, the overwhelming majority of the papers in psycho-analytic literature treat the topics of racism and prejudice as a symptom—as the external effect and social expression of internal psychological dynamics. But as Littlewood and Lipsedge (1989) said a long time a ago—"projection is a mechanism not an explanation".

The relationalists

The relationalists like Fairbairn and Winnicott shift their attention from instinct to relatedness, from breast to face, from individual to dyad. In their way of thinking, the sources of problematic adult behaviours are to be found in the particulars of the individual's developmental story. The thinking here is that people behave cruelly to others in later life because they have been dealt with cruelly in early childhood.

I would go along with this view a considerable way, but once again it is an explanation at the level of a particular individual and his or her developmental story. For this kind of explanation to work at a societal level, as would have to be the case for a phenomenon like racism, it would have to be the case that the developmental processes of a large number of members of a society must be finely synchronized. Surely this is not a realistic scenario. Further, it does not account for the occasions where racism flares up in previously convivial contexts where people have lived together for many generations.

An instance of one such theory is provided by Chasseguet-Smirgel (1990). She seeks to explain the sources of Nazism by positing the existence of a universal developmental stage that she calls the archaic oedipal matrix. According to her, when in this stage one is said to find it difficult to tolerate difference and so one seeks to merge with mother—i.e. to be the *same* as mother. But in the fullness of time the normal oedipal matrix, from which time it is possible to accommodate *difference*, supplants this matrix.

She then suggests that the German nation were for a time "stuck" in the archaic matrix, which is where Nazi ideology finds its sources. According to her, Nazi ideology is the wish for the body of the German people (the Aryans) "to become one with the body of the

Mother (the German homeland, the whole earth)" (Chasseguet-Smirgel (1990, p. 171). For this merging to proceed, the body of the German people has to be made pure—that is, homogenized—and so all differences (the Jew, the homosexual etc.) as obstacles to this union have to be purged and annihilated: "in order to form a single body, its constituent cells must be identical, purified of all foreign elements liable to impair its homogeneity" (ibid.).

As we have already noted, for this kind of theory to work at the societal level, it would have to be the case that a whole nation of individuals fell prey to the archaic matrix at about the same time, with many or most of them failing to complete the proper resolution of the complex. And then miraculously, at a certain later time, much of the nation simultaneously came to resolve the complex. The other problem with this kind theory is that it has taken it for granted that the idea of Jew is foreign, different and opposite to that of German. Some of the questions that this kind of analysis avoids are: how was it that the Jew came to be thought of as alien to a vision of German-ness? What is the ontological status of the category Aryan, from whence did it come? And so on.

Interestingly, much of psychoanalysis has been reluctant to allow the external social world a *causal* role in the structuring of internal distress, and instead, is more prone to explaining difficulties in the external social world as being due to, and driven by, distress in the internal world. For instance, Basch-Kahre (1984) says that the explanation for her black African patient's "deep feeling of being worthless whenever the theme of the stranger was brought up, [were to be found in] . . . his experience of weaning and with his oedipal conflict" (Basch-Kahre, 1984, p. 65). The fact that he was unable to advance in his job was explained completely by this *feeling* of inferiority, in other words the state of his internal world. No thought is given to the external circumstances that (a) might contribute to his inferiority, and (b) that might make it hard for him to advance. Whilst his particular experience of weaning no doubt played a significant role in the structuring of his feelings of worth-lessness, no space is given to the possibility that *components* of his worthlessness might also have to do with particular experiences of living as a black man in Sweden.

Not only does the literature tend to explain the external by the internal, it often tends to interpret engagements in the external social world as a pathology or an acting out. For example Myers (1977) understands his black female patient's increasing involvement with black militant groups as a flight from her rage with him. One could construe the patient's *new* capacity for involvement with Black militant groups as a sign of increasing health and self-esteem born of the analysis. Further, Myers reports that the patient's self-esteem does indeed increase following this involvement as revealed in her dreams. However, Myers is unable or unwilling to give *any* credit to her involvement in the external for the changes in her; he says:

> While some of this [gain] was related to modifications in the patient's self-esteem as a result of the analytic work, a good deal of it was related to her intense need to deny the underlying degraded black self-representation.

In other words her feeling better was in part "real" because of the analytic work, and in part "false" because it was due to the *repression* of her "degraded black self-representation" (Myers, 1997, p. 173).

Another instance is found in the black therapist in Holmes' (1992) description of Miss A. who was also black. Her presenting issue was a combination of "irrepressible urges" to take part in the race riots in her city. Holmes says that through the work they:

> came to understand her protestations as warded-off self-loathing which itself was in part a defence against recognition of her rage, the threatened eruption of which had brought her to treatment. [Holmes, 1992, p. 3]

Thus the political rage is understood as a displacement of the "real" internal and personal rage. It is at the very least curious that the self-loathing is *only* understood as a defence, and not as a symptom of living in a racist context.

My intention is not to dismiss internalist psychoanalytic explanations of social phenomena out of hand, but to point out their limitations. I find these ways of thinking useful and essential to my clinical work. However, when they are put forward as the *only* explanations and pose as *complete* explanations, then they lose what value they have and become dangerously reductive; in which case, they do not so much explain as explain away.

Attachment theory

Let me now turn to attachment theory. Although attachment theory in its classical form shares much common ground with the relationalists, it is distinct from them in that it places the idea of attachment prior to that of relationship. Attachment theory says that psychological relationships are generated by and through the biological processes of attachment which are themselves generated by the evolutionary processes to ensure that caregivers and their vulnerable young stay in the proximity of each other. However, attachment theory is also close to the instinctivists in that in both schemas the first impetus of the infant is generated by its biology. In a sense one could say that all three schemas are instinctivist with the differences between them being the differing aims of the instinct in each schema: for the instinctivists *per se*, to discharge; for the relationalists, to relate; and for the attachment theorists, to attach.

One need not be too afraid of the word instinct—all it means is that we are biological beings that have our evolutionary history written into our bodies. The disputes concern just what is written into the body and how fixed it is. I personally am inclined towards a stance that is akin to the relationalist, intersubjectivist and attachment schemas, rather than schemas that make hypothetical notions like the death instinct central to their cogitations.

The first thing to be said is that the "secure base" should not really be called that, it should just be called "the base"—because although one is bound to attach to it, the base is not always experienced as the source of security *per se*. Attachment theory tells us that one does not have a choice about whether to attach or not, we cannot help but attach, however vile or neglectful the base is. Imagine the torture of having to hold onto something that is too hot for comfort in order not to fall to one's death, then think of the conflicting impulses that one would have to contend with, and you would have quite a good idea of what sorts of psychological scars this kind of "attachment" experience would set up.

Problematic attachment histories lead to the generation of avoidant, ambivalent or disorganized patterns of relating to others. In these instances the attitude to others is some mix of being preoccupied with the self whilst being avoidant or/and hyper vigilant towards others. Often aggression is a means of coping with the difficulties in the internal world. These terms—avoidant, hypervigilant, aggressive and so on—are found readily in descriptions of racist phenomena. So if one were to think of racism as a pathology, as a symptom and a sign of something having gone wrong in the developmental process, then according to this kind of theory, it is here in this grouping that we would look to find its sources and genesis.

This way of thinking would suggest that securely attached persons are not likely to be racist. Felicity de Zulueta arguing from a broad relational/attachment perspective says:

> Racism . . . begins, as all acts of dehumanization, by a distortion of perception . . . This cognitive process *originates* . . . from the experience of abuse which the infant or child attempts to ward off by identifying with the aggressor . . . *the seeds of . . . racism . . . are sown in the emotional wounds of the abused and traumatized.* [de Zulueta, 1993, p. 244; italics added]

de Zulueta goes to the limit situation here to assert that racist beliefs can "*only* take [hold] . . . where the psychic template of dehumanization *already exists*" (italics added). In using the term "only", her argument is that developmental difficulties are a *necessary* condition (but not *sufficient*) for racist behaviour to occur. But if this were true, then how is it that even on the occasions when the developmental process has gone well enough, we find people behaving in racist ways? Something has escaped the analysis. I would very much agree with de Zulueta that those with problematic early attachment histories are perhaps more likely to behave in ways that we might call racist. And although I would consider her very much an ally in terms of the arguments I try to develop, my point of disagreement with her would be this: that whilst problematic developmental histories can be (and often are) contributory factors, they are neither *necessary* nor *sufficient* for racist phenomena to emerge.

I want to stress again that I do not dispute that difficulties during the early part of the developmental process will have a significant impact on possibilities and behaviours in adult life. No doubt when one probes the history of the murderous Dr Shipman (a medical doctor in the UK who killed hundreds of his elderly patients over many years), we will find events that we will say have contributed to the way he was. However, the fact that racism in the sense that I have described it, grips all peoples at different times, suggests that one needs to extend the analytic frame in order to be able to think more fully about the nature of racism. This would be something like asking, how would we set about explaining a nation of Shipmans?

It is for these sorts of reasons that it seems to me that *in its first and classical form*, attachment theory shares the same weaknesses as the relationalists, in that although the world that is taken account of is interpersonal and external, it is not yet social. The relationships and attachments that are spoken about continue to take place in a socio-logical vacuum, and further they take place between biological entities like mother, child, father, sibling, and so on.

In contrast to other schools of psychoanalysis, contemporary attachment theorists have specifically set about testing their hypoth-eses in other cultures and contexts. In doing so they acknowledge that the form and shape of the infant's developmental process is formed by and mediated through the cultural systems in which they take place. It follows then that each cultural system will generate its own forms of attachment which legitimate different ways of being together. This is akin to the multicultural ethos of respecting differ-ences, and the idea that we are equal but different and so on. But I think that one needs to go even further than this and engage with the problematic of power.

In my opinion, the schema best positioned to help us engage with the notion of power is that of Foulkesian Group Analysis, and in particular the radical version of it (Dalal, 1998, 2002).

In what follows, I will briefly introduce some group analytic thinking, and then use it to offer an elaboration of attachment theory in order to make new sense of racism.

Introducing radical group analytic thinking

I will introduce four elements from Radical Group Analytic Theory that are pertinent to the subjects under discussion, specifically from the works of the psychoanalyst and group analyst S. H. Foulkes (1948, 1964) and the sociologist Norbert Elias (1976, 1978, 1991, 1994).

The first element, power, comes via Elias. He argues that power is an inescapable aspect of all human relationships. And it is so because of the fact that as human beings we are interdependent. Interdependence is another name for "function" or "need". To say that person A has a function for person B, is to say that B needs A. If B needs A we can say that A has power "over" B. However, the reverse will also be true, but not in the same way. Hegel famously showed that the slave was not entirely powerless; the master needed the slave, even if it were only in the minimal sense of needing the slave to continue to exist in order to be exploited. One can see then that the relationship between A and B is interdependent even whilst it is bound to be asymmetric. A constrains B and *vice versa*; it is these kinds of enabling constraints that are described as power relations. Elias says that power is not a thing that one individual possesses and another does not; no one can be completely powerless or completely powerful. Power is first and last a relational attribute. Thus we can say that all relationships are of necessity power relationships.

The second element consists of a challenge to the metapsychological assumption that the social and psychological worlds are fundamentally different levels of existence. Elias dissolves this dichotomy. He is not proposing the more limited idea that these two regions influence each other—because this would be to retain an idea of the two regions as separate. He is saying something much more fundamental—that the two are aspects of the same process. Foulkes offers a helpful analogy. Imagine, we are each driving on our particular journeys. In this we are akin to autonomous individuals. But soon, we end up in a traffic jam. It now appears to each of us that there is something "outside" me that is acting "against" me, preventing me from exercising my autonomy. The name we give this kind of experience, an experience that we actually help create, sustain and remain integral to, is society.

The third element reverses the usual arrangement between the individual and social. As we have already seen, the logic of psychologies supposing that individuals are prior to society, lead them to think of the social "we" as secondary, as something that is constituted by the coming together of a number of pre-existing individual "I"s. Then it follows that forms that these societies take are said to be driven by the goings on in the internal worlds of the individuals coming together.

Radical group analysis reverses this to say that the "I" is constituted by the varieties of "we" that one is born into. Each of us, as *particular* individuals, is born into pre-existing societies constituted by a multiplicity of overlapping and conflicting cultures. The cultures themselves as well as the relationships between cultures are constituted by power relationships. As each of us "grows", we imbibe of necessity the pre-existing cultural forms, habits, beliefs and ways of thinking that we are born into. These introjections are not taken into a pre-existing self, rather they come to actually *contribute* to the formation the self. Further, because the relationships between the varieties of "we" are of necessity power relationships, then we can say that the "I", the "me", is constituted at the deepest of levels by and through the power relationships that are part of the social fabric that one is born into.

Foulkes is not espousing a kind of social determinism in which human beings are mere pawns of social forces. As will become clear, to think in this way does not mean that one is denying the existence of individuals each with their *unique* sense of self, or denying that they are biological beings in bodies.

The fourth element concerns the notion of belonging. Foulkes asserts that there is a fundamental need in all human beings to belong—to be part of an "us"—and that this is a *necessary* condition for an experience of psychological well-being. But even to put it in this way, to say that there is a need to belong, misrepresents the situation, as it implies that there is the possibility of not belonging. It is the case that we cannot not-belong.

I will now return to attachment theory.

Socializing attachment theory

The ideas I have introduced via radical group analytic theory are not unfamiliar to contemporary attachment theorists—for example, Peter Fonagy and Jeremy Holmes.

Fonagy says that the child comes to form its sense of self through internalizing the picture in the parent's mind of the child's state of mind. He says that this is the mechanism through which the child comes "to form the core sense of himself" (Fonagy, 2001, p. 175).

However, the mother does not just experience a baby *per se*, but a particular kind of baby. She, like all of us, will be led to particular ways of experiencing the world according to the conventions written into the discourses we inhabit. For example it is a well-established fact that caregivers tend to treat male offspring more favourably than female ones. This kind of finding is further substantiated by studies of the amount of attention school teachers give their male and female pupils, where it is found that even whilst the teachers imagine that they are giving equal amounts to each, the males get more. On another theme, it is not uncommon for darker skinned children to be less welcomed than lighter skinned children in many Asian and Afro-Caribbean families.

I do not wish to suggest that all female and darker skinned infants would be universally, uniformly and inevitably denigrated—as this would be a form of social determinism; an idea that I do not sign up to. One reason that things are not so fixed is that we inhabit multiple discourses at the same time; discourses that continually contest and subvert each other. But the point is that we are never outside discourses; we are never in an ideology free zone.

It seems to me that the caregiver gives back to the infant something much more than a picture of *the infant's state of mind* as it exists in *the caregiver's mind*. The caregiver is also giving back to the infant the caregiver's *attitude* to the infant, which comes in turn to inform the growing infant's attitude towards itself. Another name for one's attitude towards oneself is *self esteem*. The key thing is that the attitudes of the caregiver are severely constrained by the discourses that have formed the caregivers themselves. These attitudes being unreflected, are outside the scope of consciousness; indeed it is what allows our consciousness to take the forms that it does. Foulkes calls this taken for granted ground that *forms* our response, thoughts and experiences, the social unconscious.

A similar view is found in attachment theory too. Liotti (1987) calls these schemata "super conscious" rather than unconscious, and says that they are the organizing principles "which govern the conscious processes without appearing in them" (cited in Holmes, 1993, p. 170).

What I am arguing is that the image of the self that the infant takes in from its caregivers is from the first, intrinsically social, by which I mean that the infant is never just an infant *per se* to itself, but a particular infant who, by virtue of its attributes, finds itself situated and positioned in the caregiver's affections, and so comes eventually to similarly situate and position itself.

This means that one may no longer make a dichotomy between a social self and a personal/true self, because the personal self is intrinsically social. The philosopher David Hume was onto something similar when he speculated that there was no such thing as a self outside, beyond or prior to the attributes that one can name about the self.

This way of thinking, in which the external social world and the things that actually go on between people are given a fundamentally formative role in the creation of what takes place in the so called internal world of individuals, is anathema to certain psychoanalytic orthodoxies, who tend to give developmental primacy to a notion of phantasy over lived experience. Clinical training grounded in these traditions train novices to read their patient's descriptions of actual enacted events as signs and ciphers pointing to the workings of the psychological world. If the therapist treats these descriptions more straightforwardly (by which I don't mean a naïve acceptance) by having a causal role in their own right, then it is taken to be the case that the therapist has been seduced by the patient, and has capitulated in some way. This world view has a very powerful grip on our profession, so much so that even the analysts that give credence and weight to the so-called external differences, such as colour, tend to talk of these differences being used as defences by the patient, and successful therapies as moving past these external differences to some deeper level, to engage with the "real" person behind these categories.

This attention paid to the lived external world, is one of the main reasons why attachment theory is viewed with such hostility and contempt by sections of certain orthodoxies in psychoanalysis.

In the foregoing, I have been working towards the idea that the so-called social categories of identity (in general) are integral to the deep sense of self, the experience of the "true me".

If we accept this, then it follows that in attaching to persons we are also, of necessity, attaching to categories, however subliminal our sense of them might be.

Actually, attachment is not a strong enough word because it suggests a picture in which two pre-existing selves come secondarily to attach to each other. But what is actually being suggested and described by Fonagy, Foulkes and others is the radical idea that there is no self prior to the processes of attachment and introjection, and that the infant's self is constructed through the attachment processes themselves. To restate this in group analytic language would be to say that who I am is the same as where I belong.

We can see then why it is that when the social identities one finds oneself imbued with are trampled on, tampered with, trivialized, denigrated or dismissed in some way, it affects one so powerfully. One is likely to experience such moments as attacks on one's integrity, as a violation of the sanctity of one's being.

To reinforce the point: we do not just attach to people, but also attach to categories. However, in speaking in this way it makes it appear that things in the internal world are more fixed than they actually are.

Making a difference

The preceding discussion has rendered the world too simple on two further counts: first, it takes the categories of belonging such as White, Moslem, and so on, to be facts straightforwardly existing out there in the world. Second, the categories have been spoken of as though they were homogenous unities.

I will unpack these simplifications and begin with two premises: (1) that we cannot *not attach*, and we cannot *not belong*: and (2) attachment and belonging are aspects of the same process.

The idea of belonging is paradoxical in that for the experience of belonging to be meaningful, two conditions have to be fulfilled: first, in order to belong to one thing it is necessary for there to be something else *not* to belong to. Second, it has to be the case that only some may belong, and others are not allowed to belong. If these two conditions are not fulfilled then the belonging category becomes infinitely large encompassing everything and everybody, and so becomes meaningless.

In other words intrinsic to the ideas of attaching and belonging is the *negation* of something and someone. Donald Winnicott (1965, p. 149), said something similar when he described the infant's first

"I am" moment in which it gathers itself together, as a paranoid moment. This is because as the infant gathers some elements together from the environment to form itself, it simultaneously repudiates other elements. In a sense the infant is saying to the "not-me" elements: "you don't belong". Having made this gesture, the infant now fears attack from the repudiated elements; hence the paranoia. Winnicott suggests that "we" groups come about through a very similar mechanism—the repudiation of the elements designated "not-we"; or to put it another way, a "we" can exist *only* as a contrast to a "them". Or to put it another way again, even as one makes a gesture of inclusion in one direction, in the very same moment, one cannot help but make a gesture of exclusion to every other direction.

I will try to make things a bit clearer through two well-known jokes that are really parables.

A woman gives her husband two ties. When she sees him wearing one of them she exclaims: "So you did not like the other." When I was first told this, the moral of the story that I was invited to draw was that in choosing one thing we are not necessarily condemning the other. But over time, I have come to think that a negation of some sort is in fact taking place, precisely because in that moment one has been chosen over the other. The two ties are different *and not equal*.

The second joke: A devout orthodox Jew found himself marooned on an uninhabited island. When he was rescued many years later by a passing ship, the rescuers were astonished to see that he had built himself a synagogue to worship in. But then as they rounded the island, they were further astonished to see yet another synagogue. Mystified, they asked the castaway why he had built two synagogues. He replied that one was the synagogue that he went to, and the other was the synagogue that he did not go to.

Fortified by these parables, I will now go a little further again.

It is the case that it is impossible to say just what is the essence of a particular "us", say, "Britishness". When we look directly at the British "us", we find not homogeneity but heterogeneity: vegetarians, whites, landlords, Kleinians, Scots, blacks, football hooligans, accountants, Christians, Moslems, fascists, liberals, and so on. And if one turns one's attention to each of these sub-groupings, they too dissolve into further arrays of diversity. I think that it is precisely because of the impossibility to find and name the essence of the "us" that one looks to the margins, to the "not-us".

The "us" is defined not so much by what it is, but by what it is not. The structuralist De Sassure (1959) said pretty much the same thing. He said:

> concepts are purely differential and defined not by their positive content but negatively by their relations with the other terms of the system. Their most precise characteristic is in being what others are not. [De Sassure, 1959, p. 117]

It is also the case that there is no unity to be found in the not-us either. In sum, the impression of difference and Otherness between the "us" and "them" is as illusory as is the impression of solidity and cohesion within the "us" and "them". However, the illusions are powerful nonetheless, and come to have a life as facts in our psyches as well as our engagements with each other. They come to have a particular kind of reality.

Given the fragility of each of these belongings, as well as the fact that there are an infinity of alternative belongings continually available to each of us, prompts the question: how and why do we come to experience one encounter as taking place across a difference and the other as within a region of similarity? What leads us to assert that the therapy taking place between Mr Smith and Mr Singh is multicultural whilst that between Mr Smith and Mr Jones is not? As we already noted earlier, it is possible to frame both encounters in terms of similarity as well as difference.

The answers, I would say, are not to do with the nature of the differences themselves, but with the *functions* the processes of differentiation are being required to perform. This is the "why" question that I flagged up earlier. It is not the case that one simply "finds" a difference, which one then finds oneself responding to. *Rather, one finds oneself emphasizing certain differences in order to create a differentiation.* The questions one needs constantly to ask are: Given that there are an infinity of differences (and similarities) between two human beings, how and why are we led in a particular moment to experience and construe one difference primary and render the others less meaningful? What and importantly, *whose* purpose is being served by making the differentiation here rather than there?

My argument is this: differences are evoked *in order to make a differentiation*, and even more specifically, a differentiation between the haves and the must-not-haves.

The point is that all societies, all cultures, are not homogeneities but structures of power relations in which different groupings—each with their own agendas and beliefs—contest each other. The Brahmin and the Untouchable experience very different kinds of Hindu culture. Now, it is precisely because of the fluidity of the boundaries there is the ever present danger of one sort of "us" dissolving and reorganizing into another sort of "us"; and so continual work is required to shore up and bolster the "us". This work takes several forms. One bit of the work is done for us silently and automatically by our cognitive mechanisms. Social scientists have demonstrated that when the mind uses an attribute to make groupings out of continuities, there follows a kind of hallucination in which it seems to us that those within each of the groupings appear to be more similar than they actually are, and that the gap between the groupings appears to be greater than it actually is. This cognitive hallucination is necessary for the formation and experience of categories.

But this is not nearly enough and so the emotions are called into play to help maintain the distance between the "us" and varieties of "them". The primary mechanism is one where the "them" are denigrated and the "us" are idealized. The notions of denigration and idealization, being absolute (good and only good, bad and only bad), create the impression of an antithetical dichotomy between the "us" and the "them"—a dichotomy with a chasm between them. *In other words it has created the illusion of types.*

One of the most prodigious of these illusory typologies is the one we call race.

But what is race?

Whatever race is, it is used to sort varieties of human kinds. Implicit to this possibility is the apparent truism that *there are indeed different kinds of humans to be sorted.* But in fact when one tries to examine the notion of race, it disintegrates. The attempts to define and distinguish race (physiology) from culture (behaviour and belief) from ethnicity (internal sense of belonging) continually fail, as the attempted definitions of each continually collapse into each other.

Bailey's definition is a particularly telling one: "The term '*Ethnic*

Minority' is much debated but includes a wide variety of *races* and *culture* both *black* and *white*" (Bailey 1996, p. 89; italics added).

This failure to make and sustain a distinction between the three terms flags up the idea that there is something problematic with this way of dividing humanity. However, curiously, notions of black and white have been used from the first to name all three categories—we talk easily of black and white races, cultures and ethnicities. This thought serves as a prompt to shift our attention onto the notions of black and white.

Because of the time restrictions I cannot build my arguments up as carefully as I would like to. The detailed work behind what I am about to say can be found in my books.

Is it not curious that the peoples that we call black and white are not actually chromatically black and white? How do they come to be so named? Through tracing the semantic history of the words black and white in the English language, one discovers that the words start off relatively neutral. The diagram on page 30, *The evolving meanings of black and white*, shows that over the last millennium the terms black and white increasingly gather associations of negativity and positivity, respectively. There are two periods in which there are dramatic bursts of new associations, the Middle Ages—the time of the Crusades, and from the 16th Century onwards—the beginnings of the Imperial adventure.

It is surprising to discover how recent so many of these associations are. The association of black with dirt was first recorded in 1300 AD, with death in 1400 AD, immorality in 1552 AD, with evil in 1581 AD. Eventually, things that can have no colour like the negative emotions start being called black from the 17th Century onwards. This last point is a particularly telling one. What it is showing is that as the world is becoming increasingly colour coded, so is the psyche.

There is a double movement here: on the one hand the attaching of black to a thing lends that thing a negative valence and so impels one to push it away, on the other hand things imbued with negativity are increasingly perceived as "naturally" having something black about them. The conclusion I draw is that blackness gets attached to a thing *in order* to cathect it with repellence, with the converse being true of whiteness. For example, it is surprising to discover that in the English language, the "Black Plague" which took place in the 13th Century, was first called the *Black* Plague in the 19th Century.

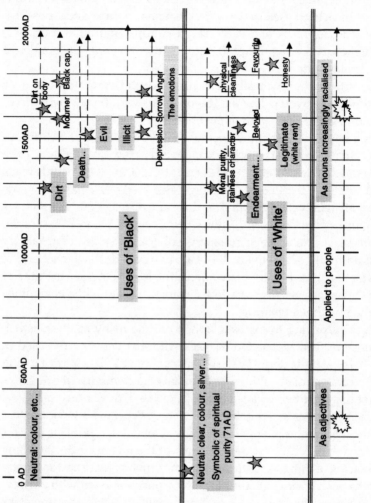

The evolving meaning of black and white

Similarly, the Black Prince was first so called two hundred years after his death. It is my contention that over this epoch, notions of white and black became honed into powerful tools used to lever things into the territories designated as good or bad, in or out, us or them. They became instruments of inclusion and exclusion.

The hollowness of race as a category, is one of the reasons that it has come to rely on something apparently more substantial (notions of black and white) to sustain itself.

Black and White are first used to *name* races—that is as *nouns* for people of different types in the 16th Century. By this time the words have already been loaded up with many of the associations they are to bear. Thus the naming of people black and white is not so much a descriptive act, but an "Othering" process—a racializing process. Something very similar is taking place even with the seemingly more innocuous terms culture and ethnicity. It is no coincidence that people who designated themselves as "white" first gave the people designated as black, their name "black".

But there is no "done deal" here either. There were enormous debates and struggles as to whether the Irish were to be admitted to the category white, as was also the case for the southern Europeans.

One of the troubles with the notion of race is that people tend to take its existence to be fact, and then use the thing called "race" to be in itself the source and the explanation for racism. Why were there riots in Chicago or Bradford? Answer: because of racial difference. The solution offered by the multiculturalists is to invite us to "tolerate" difference. Meanwhile some socio-biologists explain away the situation through a four stage argument based on the idea of the selfish gene.

They begin with the assertion that we are programmed by the evolutionary processes to act in ways that will enhance the chances of our genes surviving and multiplying. Next, we are said to share more genes with kin than those not-kin, and this makes us automatically favour kin over others. Third, ethnicity or race is said to be an extension of kinship, and so we are said to naturally favour those of the same race or ethnic group over others. And finally, when we behave in these "natural" ways—then we are accused of being racist.

Here are some of the flaws in their argument: any human grouping is found to have approximately 15 per cent of its DNA patterns in common. This means that the other 85 per cent is shared with the rest of humanity. So why should this 15 per cent seek to favour its kin and not the other 85 per cent? It is also the case that we share 98 per cent of our DNA with chimpanzees—yet we do not treat them too well. And finally, we need go back only 150,000 years to find one of the common ancestors for all of human kind—thus in a very real sense, we are all kin.

We are forced back to the perplexing question: if there are no races then what is racism? It seems to me that the only way to answer this is to say that racism is anything—thought, feeling or action—that uses the notion of race as an activating or organizing principle. Or to put it another way, *racism is the manufacture and use of the notion of race.*

One can see that this definition of racism is one of *activity*; thus I would say that more useful than the notion of racism is that of *racialization*—the process of manufacturing and utilizing the notion of race in any capacity.

The fact that we inhabit a racialized and colour coded world, means that through the psycho-social developmental process, each of us, of necessity, imbibes a version of that world order, such that our psyches too become colour-coded and racialized. And then we in turn continue to reproduce and sustain the processes of racialization despite ourselves.

Processes of Othering

Fonagy said poetically: "At the core of the mature child's self is the other at the moment of reflection" (Fonagy, 2001, p. 173).

But this "other" at the core of the self is not really "other" because by definition, it is part of the self. And being part of the self one recognizes the other in the self and the self in the other. Perhaps another term for this kind of recognition is empathy. To my mind empathy is another way of thinking about these benign forms of attachment.

Now, whatever racism is, it is essentially a dehumanizing process, through which "an other" is transformed into "The Other", from one of "us" into one of "them". The racialized and dehumanized Other is positioned outside the moral universe with all its attendant requirements and obligations to fellow human beings.

However, one of the things I have been arguing for previously is that Strangers are not found but made—we estrange them. This act of Othering, or estranging, in part consists of the activity of repressing, subjugating and annihilating the similarities between self and Other; the ways in which the other is known and understood.

One could call this a detaching process, the process through which differences are named and amplified in order to simultaneously create and detach from a "them". Anything can be alighted on, and once alighted, then it seems ever so natural that that difference is anathema to us. Recall, in Gulliver's Travels two nations differentiated themselves and went to war on the basis of which end of a boiled egg should be broken into first.

In this arena, the purpose of naming a difference is to make a division between the haves and the must-not-haves. When one difference weakens in this task, we amplify others. For example:

Tales told by early European adventurers during the late Middle Ages described the Africans in language we would today call racist. However they did not use the word race. To my mind this was because they did not need to as they were thought of as something not quite human. The notion of race made its entry at the point that it became clear that they were in fact part of humanity. Now what was said that they might be human but they are of a different race. As the notion of race crumbled, the notion of culture was brought to the fore; what is said now is that we are all the same race, but have different cultures. And finally, ethnicity makes its entry when it becomes hard to sustain a meaningful distinction between cultural groupings—say Hindus and Moslems in India, or Jews and Arabs in the Middle East. The terms change from race to culture to ethnicity, but the work remains the same.

The fact is that the Othering process is a work that is continually being done, because there is the ever present danger that some of "them" will become "us". In part this work consists of creating and maintaining a buffer of hatred, disgust and contempt. But the fact that this work requires a continual engagement with "them" in order to estrange "them", then perhaps the idea of detachment does not actually capture all of what is going on.

In order for a "we" to exist, the "we" need a "them" to continue to exist but at a distance. Thus the "we" needs to be continually in touch with the "them" paradoxically in order to keep the "them" at a distance. Could we say then that this kind of paradoxical keeping in touch/distancing is also a form of attachment? If we go down this road then could we say that hate too is a form of attachment?

The predicaments we have to continually live and contend with are manifold: first, we cannot not divide; second, in order to belong and be included, we are obliged to in that same existential moment to exclude; third, the places we divide are by no means natural, however self evident they might appear at times.

I will end with a quote from Elias:

> [in] discussing 'racial' problems one is apt to put the cart before the horse. It is argued, as a rule, that people perceive others as belonging to another group because the colour of their skin is different. It would be more to the point if one asked how it came to pass in this world that one has got into the habit of perceiving people with another skin colour as belonging to a different group. [Elias, 1976: xlvii]

I hope that I have begun to answer the question of how it came to pass that we got into the habit of perceiving people with another skin colour as belonging to a different group—and then indeed—of treating them differently.

Note

Some material for this article is drawn from a book by the author, *Race, Colour and the Process of Racialization: New Perspectives from Group Analysis, Psychoanalysis and Sociology* (Dalal, 2002).

References

Bailey, C. (1996). The health needs of children from ethnic minorities. In: K. N. Dwivedi, & V. P. Varma, (Eds), *Meeting the Needs of Ethnic Minority Children*, pp. 89–95. London: Jessica Kingsley.

Basch-Kahre, E. (1984). On difficulties arising in transference and counter transference when analyst and analysand have different socio-cultural backgrounds. *International Review of Psychoanalysis, 11*: 61–67.

Chasseguet-Smirgel, J. (1990). Reflections of a Psychoanalyst upon the Nazi Biocracy and Genocide. *International Review of Psychoanalysis*, 17: 167–175.

Dalal, F. (1998). *Taking the Group Seriously—Towards a Post Foulkesian Group Analytic Theory*. London: Jessica Kingsley.

Dalal, F. (2002). *Race, Colour and the Processes of Racialization*. Hove: Routledge.

Elias, N. (1976). Introduction. In: N. Elias and J. Scotson (1994), *The Established and the Outsiders*. London: Sage.

Elias, N. (1978). *What is Sociology?* New York: Columbia University Press.

Elias, N. (1991). *The Symbol Theory*. London: Sage.

Elias, N. (1994). *The Civilizing Process*. Oxford: Blackwell.

Fairbairn, R. (1935). The social significance of communism considered in the light of psychoanalysis. In: R. Fairbairn (1994), *Psychoanalytic Studies of the Personality*. London: Routledge.

Foulkes, S. H. (1948). *Introduction to Group Analytic Psychotherapy*. London: Heinemann, reprinted 1983 London: Karnac Books.

Foulkes, S. H. (1964). *Therapeutic Group Analysis*. London: George Allen & Unwin.

Fonagy, P. (2001). *Attachment Theory and Psychoanalysis*, London: Karnac.

Holmes D. E. (1992). Race and transference in psychoanalysis and psychotherapy. *International Journal of Psychoanalysis*, 73: 1–11.

Holmes, J. (1993). *John Bowlby and Attachment Theory*. London: Routledge.

Klein, M. (1959). Our adult world and its roots in infancy. In: M. Klein (1988), *Envy and Gratitude and Other Works*, 1946–1963. London: Virago.

Littlewood, R., & Lipsedge, M. (1989). *Aliens and Alienists—Ethnic Minorities and Psychiatry*. London: Unwin Hyman.

Myers, W. A. (1977). The significance of the colors black and white in the dreams of black and white patients. *Journal of American Psychoanalytic Association*, 25: 163–181.

de Saussure, F. (1959). *Course in General Linguistics*. New York: The Philosophical Library.

Winnicott, D. W. (1965). *The Family and Individual Development*. London: Tavistock Publications.

de Zulueta F. (1993). *From Pain to Violence—The Traumatic Roots of Destructiveness*. London: Whurr.

Revisiting the concepts of racism and culture: Some thoughts on the clinical implications

A response to Farhad Dalal's paper

Zack Eleftheriadou

Introduction

The primary aim of this paper is to revisit the concepts of "race" and "culture" and expand current thinking using research findings from the fields of child psychology and social psychology. I argue that in order to understand the cross-cultural relationship, we need to incorporate a psychosocial framework. A clinical case study of work with a child will be used to discuss the clinical implications.

Revisiting the concepts of "race" and "culture"

This paper will begin with the premise that the concept "race" is invalid; it is not a biological reality and in Vannoy-Adams' (1996) terms, we can view it as a "psychical reality". It is worth examining the extensive study by the cross-cultural psychologist, Professor Marshall Segal, entitled: "All of Us are Related, Each of Us is Unique". He states:

This exhibition is designed to contribute to contemporary discourse on human diversity. It is a graphic presentation of biological findings rooted in genetics research, and it includes striking displays of phenotypical variations, conventionally thought to be categorical. In fact, they are continuous.

Dramatically, via evidence on human migrations and adaptations, the exhibition shows how erroneous conventional wisdom has been with respect to the deeply ingrained concept of discrete "races". [Segal, 2002, p. 1]

The original, French-language version of the exhibition, entitled "Tous Parents, Tous Différents", was produced in the Department of Genetic Anthropology in Geneva, Switzerland and is on continuous display at the Musée de L'Homme in Paris.

In fact, it is more useful to refer to "racism", or what happens when race categories are used to determine people's behaviours. Racism is the process by which people are made to be invisible, by ignoring their needs, making them subordinate and portraying them only through stereotypes. Aronson defines stereotypes as:

... based on hearsay or images concocted by the mass media or are generated within our heads as ways of justifying our own prejudices and cruelty. [Aronson, 1984, p. 230]

As Farhad Dalal has stated in his paper entitled "Racism: Processes of Detachment, Dehumanization and Hatred", we have multiple racial groupings and the racial "us" versus "not-us" grouping does not have clear boundaries, they are fluid categories. Keeping in mind its fluidity and how perceptions change within different environments is vital. I think it is useful to broaden the concept of race and to consider, in addition, the concepts of "ethnicity" (or "belongingness") or "culture". However, we must remain cautious that we have not replaced race with the word culture, to refer to something equally rigid.

Culture is not a rigid or closed system of ideas. It is a flexible construction of the world to which a certain group of people belong, which is geographically and historically specific. [Eleftheriadou, 1994, p. 2]

It includes all the observable as well as subtle aspects, such as communication, nuances, relationship patterns, religion, and spirituality amongst many others, which are meaningful to a group. Often we see these differences as unchangeable, as if they are indeed genetic. An individual can identify with a racial grouping as their primary identity; for example, "*I identify myself as black or white*" or a religious/cultural identity, for example "*I am Muslim or Catholic*".

We all hold several different identities at the same time, but "developing a healthy racial/ethnic racial identity is a central component of one's overall self–concept" (Ponterotto and Pedersen, 1993, p. 62). As a supervisor, I am often amazed how little racial/cultural material therapists gather within the therapeutic arena. It really brings into question the responsibility we have, as therapists, to address these issues and support clients who hold stereotypical or in some ways fragile racial identities. Of course, I am not implying that all our clients hold fragile racial identities. However, in order to connect properly with our clients, racial/cultural material still needs to be brought in to the therapeutic relationship, even with clients who have a strong sense of their racial/cultural identity.

Child development

From an attachment perspective, young children receive conscious and unconscious psychosocial cues initially from their parents. This process determines the nature of the child's exploration of the environment and will play a crucial part in shaping their own psycho-racial identity. In healthy development, the "secure base" may motivate the child to explore, in order to find something to become attached to, seeking something which is safe and containing. When there is repeated hostility, people develop selective information gathering about other groups, and seek out only information that will validate their perceptions. The case becomes more complex when a child is brought up in more than one environment, has a dual heritage or is adopted, where one cannot simply close off contact with one racial group. This is a parallel process for the immigrant or the ethnic minority community.

Groupings and territorial behaviour begin very early on. Children from around 3–4 years old demonstrate ethnic awareness, as they begin to engage in more interactive play. They can look at pictures or dolls and state whether they are the same as them or different, but they tend to be clearer on the more obvious black and white differences. Apart from these early identifications and social groupings, there is also the beginning of some level of ethnic prejudice (Durkin, 1995). The dynamics of placing aggression on something that is frightening and must be conquered or seen as inferior and must be controlled (both of these are interlinked of course), are already at play. In some cases, the focus of the child's prejudices is likely to reflect the status of one's own group (Tajfel, 1981). However, as we are not just recipients of social pressures, children do not always simply replicate the views of their parents, and the nature and intensity of children's prejudices change with age, as cognitive processes become more sophisticated. (Aboud, 1988). Furthermore, within one social grouping one does not necessarily find consistency in its preferences or the ways it discriminates against other groups.

A consistent research finding is that minority children often show a preference towards other groups and reject their own (Durkin, 1995). In my clinical experience, I have certainly come across children who want to change their skin colour from black to white, not black to Indian or Italian for example. Children feel what is being projected onto them, even if it is not made explicit. A powerful example comes from the main character, Hyacinth, who in Joan Riley's book *The Unbelonging*, eloquently describes her experiences, such as being looked at with "suspicion and dislike" or seeing the hate in people's faces (Riley, 1985, p. 68). I will continue on this theme with a case study of a young child in therapy. (To maintain confidentiality identifying details have been changed.)

Case study: Ben

Ben was referred to me after being extremely disruptive at school, unable to concentrate and would often get into fights. The therapist had felt that this 9 year old boy was so full of rage and held himself in such poor self-esteem, that he needed the space to work through things in individual psychotherapy. He came from a dual heritage background, a partnership that had only lasted a few years between a black Afro-Caribbean man and a white British woman. In the last year his mother had remarried a white man. His father had another partner, also from a dual heritage background, and they had two children, a boy and a girl. Ben maintained regular, but infrequent contact with his father.

From the beginning, Ben found it difficult to be close to anyone and had to fight everything. He would often say that I was taking up his precious play time, and extending boring school time. His drawings were full of battles between weak and strong, frightening looking creatures who would continually fight. When it appeared that one had died, it would somehow re-emerge or change form.

After returning from the summer break, he said he did not want to talk about "stuff that goes on in your head, that's just boring". At this point we could hear people in the street, talking in an animated way. He half shouted to them "well, you are just a f. . . .ing packi, aren't you?," this continued with other racial abuse of Indians, adding "you are just stupid man, no brain". He laughed out loud about this. I was in touch with so much sadness about him at this point. He looked up at me and said, in a rather cheeky manner, "you are not offended are you?", expecting quite a reaction from me. He said I bet other kids you see don't say stuff like that. Already we were getting into my other kids and his fantasies of them.

I explored his comments to the passers by, as a way of venting some of his own rage in response to the racial abuse that he had received and that he was now placing it onto others (knowing of course that they were likely to have experienced being treated similarly). I also explored his curiosity about how would I react hearing racial comments like that and his wondering whether I would really ever understand what it felt like to be a boy with his background. From my original appointment letter, he had already thought I wasn't going to understand him because "I would be white and not like him". Our preconceptions, or what has been called "pre-transference" or "societal transference", about the therapist's racial and cultural background come into the therapeutic encounter before the therapeutic couple have even met. We project our everyday social experiences onto the therapeutic situation. For someone like Ben, who was experiencing racial abuse frequently and unclear racial/cultural messages from his parents, it was natural that on some level he would expect to receive the same from me.

However, in this session he said, *"actually, I knew you weren't 'white' from your name, but did not think where you were from. Now I wonder whether you are kind of mixed too"*. Suddenly, we were not as distant as in the previous weeks and I felt I had touched on something painful. He then told me how *"kids say stuff like that on the bus every day, but don't worry, they just get used to this"*. I said that maybe that's what made it difficult and made him more and more furious in that you never get used to stuff like that and that you shouldn't get used to stuff like that because it hurts and it's unfair to be called things without anyone really knowing you. He became increasingly subdued as the session went on and eventually in tears, he recalled to me bullying incidents on the bus home from school. They called his mother names for having a relationship with a black man and said that they had never seen his father around anyway. He used to wish his father would just turn up and show them.

He told me for the first time that it all just made him feel so confused. He described everything in his mother's house as "white", for example, the food and their friends and that they did not know anything about the Caribbean. He did not look like any of them. Of course he had also felt left out with his mother's new husband. On the other hand, he did not really know his father and he feared his temper. Nothing had ever happened to him, but he always feared *"getting it wrong"*. We ended up writing all his different identities on paper, almost like a pie chart, trying to bring some integration. He then left saying, *"I will think about it and guess by next week where you are from"*, and rushed out. I was relieved that it was finally safer to talk about his experiences rather than being in touch with his rage, which could be so out of control and be thrown onto any target, like the passers by in the street. We were finally talking about our own relationship and he was going to take something with him for reflection.

I chose this case because with kids, racial/cultural material is more readily available and yet there is also such immaturity about how to understand it all. Ben felt he did not belong at home and had to cope with racial abuse and bullying at school. He had had a difficult upbringing anyway with a mother that saw him as the spitting image of his father and a father who was rarely around. There were many complicated themes, but for the purposes of this paper I will summarize the main themes that emerged:

1. The various battles he had witnessed between the parental couple, often extremely aggressive;
2. The black and white heritage inside him that he just could not and had had no help, to integrate, as well as how this had become intensified by the bullying and racism at school;
3. The battles with his mother, usually about school and his behaviour;
4. The more subtle clashes with his father, with whom he could not be in touch nor show his anger towards, as he feared his father's rejection.

There are many aspects I could address, but the one essential point to make is that he needed me to hear and validate his experiences and not interpret the racism as only taking place towards him. Similarly, if I had only interpreted the parental dynamics and not the rest of the racial and cultural meanings we would have missed other significant social experiences. Unconscious transference dynamics can only be worked with when we can tolerate racial and cultural difference at a deep level, which can only take place if we have undertaken a great deal of personal exploration of these issues. Vannoy-Adams (1996), describes the fear of being supplanted by the other, and this fear or panic being so great that one can avoid the other completely. The person may try to dominate, instead of being dominated. Of course these are the more extreme defensive responses and there are also in-between states. He develops this argument further describing the "plural psyche" as not the one that tries to merge all the elements together, but the one that can hold all the racial/cultural tensions together.

Social psychology

Psychoanalysis has provided us with theories and exploratory tools, but I feel strongly we also need to look outside these intrapsychic theories (see also Farhad Dalal's and Kimberlyn Leary's papers in this volume). I think social psychology is able to shed a great deal of light on our understanding of racism as it is a social construct, created by groups of people in order to include and exclude. Social psychology research has shown, how individuals can behave, often in shocking ways, when they are placed in groups and their sense of individual responsibility diminishes.

One of the most studied areas is aggression. Social psychologists define aggression as an interplay between inherent characteristics and learned responses and I think the same applies to the process of racism. In the groundbreaking book *The Social Animal* it was shown that:

> Most individuals must dehumanize their victims in order to commit an extreme act of aggression, then, by building empathy among people; aggressive acts will become more difficult to commit. [Aronson, 1984, p. 224]

This was evident in the case of Ben, described above, who could safely place his own racism onto passers by as they were strangers. Similarly, Feshback (1969) showed that children will demonstrate less aggression when they empathise more with the person. It is worth mentioning the example of the 1960's experiment by Muzafer Sherif and his colleagues (see Aronson, 1984). They divided 14-year-old boys into two teams and it only took a short time for them to become highly aggressive with each other. The behaviour towards each other improved dramatically only when they had to cooperate as a team. For example, they were placed in pretend emergency situations, like having to deal with a damaged water supply system, where they had to work towards a common goal. Freud, who only discussed racial issues briefly, said something extremely illuminating on this issue, that

> it is precisely the minor differences in people who are otherwise alike that form the basis of feelings of strangeness and hostility between them. [Freud, 1984: (11) 199]

He explained this as a form of narcissism.

The research findings I have mentioned have significant implications for therapeutic work. These include the importance of allowing adequate space for our clients to explore these highly emotive issues, bringing them into the therapeutic setting and addressing them as part of the relationship, so they do not remain something that is externalized as "out there" and out of mind. The notion of therapeutic empathy has to incorporate racial, cultural or "other" empathy. We can only go there with our clients, if we have allowed ourselves to go through this process personally, through cross-cultural supervision as well as group experiences which address race and cultural issues.

As Erich Fromm (1976), stated we have a basic human need for belongingness and rootedness. In seeking this while in defensive states and groupings, we may end up creating a "cognitive hallucination", which Farhad Dalal discusses in his paper. This is where social groupings perceive themselves to be more similar than they are.

Conclusion

Like Farhad Dalal, I hope that I have highlighted the complexity of analysing racial and cultural issues. As soon as one tries to pin down the notion of race, we can end up reinforcing its existence. Psycho-analysis has come a long way, but still has much work to do in refining theory and examining the clinical implications, especially in working with cross-cultural populations. The clinical work and writings of people like Kimberlyn Leary, Farhad Dalal, Jaffar Kareem, Roland Littlewood and Vannoy Adams have made significant contributions to our thinking and practice. We need theory and research from individual, group, and social psychology as well as the clinical insights of psychoanalysis to provide a clearer picture of these powerful racial dynamics. In addition, there is much for educators and clinicians to learn about how to intervene at different developmental stages by considering the findings from research in child development.

In order to work with these issues clinically, we do need to work with differences and similarities at the same time (Eleftheriadou, 1994). That is to say that there are unique racial/cultural elements and there are universal human needs and struggles.

I would like to end with another quote from Jaffar Kareem (1992), who stated:

I believe racism is not simply a black or white problem. It is a human problem and one which includes all human beings and as such the struggle against racism cannot be separated from other struggles for human dignity and individual freedom. [Kareem, 1992, p. 25]

References

Aboud, F. E. (1988). *Children and Prejudice*. London: Blackwell.

Aronson, E. (1984). *The Social Animal* (4th Edn). New York: W. H. Freeman.

Barrett, M., & Short, J. (1992). Images of European people in a group of 5- to 10-year-old English school children. *British Journal of Developmental Psychology, 10*: 339–363.

Durkin, K. (1995). *Developmental Social Psychology*. London: Blackwell.

Eleftheriadou, Z. (1994). *Transcultural Counselling*. London: Central Books.

Feshback, S. (1971). Dynamics and morality of violence and aggression: Some psychological considerations. *American Psychologist, 26*: 281–292.

Feshback, N., & Feshback, S. (1969). The relationship between empathy and aggression in two age groups. *Developmental Psychology, 1*: 102–107.

Freud, S. (1984). *Metapsychology—The theory of Psychoanalysis (Volume 11)*. Harmondsworth: Penguin.

Fromm. E. (1976). *To Have or To Be?* New York: Harper and Row.

Kareem, J., & Littlewood, R. (1992). *Intercultural Therapy*. London: Blackwell.

Ponterotto, J. G., Pedersen, P. (1993). *Preventing Prejudice*. London: Sage.

Riley, J. (1985). *The Unbelonging*. London: The Women's Press.

Segal, M. (2002). *All of Us are Related, Each of Us is Unique*. New York: Syracuse University. (http://allrelated.syr.edu/index.html)

Tajfel, H. (1981). *Human Groups and Social Categories: Studies in Social Psychology*. Cambridge: Cambridge University Press.

Vannoy-Adams, M. (1996). *The Multicultural Imagination: "Race", Colour and the Unconscious*. London: Routledge.

Difference

Cascia Davis

W hen I was invited to take part in the conference I was both nervous and excited. In thinking about what I would present, nothing came—no thoughts or ideas. Some weeks later, not consciously thinking about what I might write these words came to mind:

> I woke up this morning and I was me,
> I went downstairs, ate breakfast and I was me.
> I went through the front door and I was different.
> What is the difference?
> What caused the difference?
> Is it just me who is different?
> Or are we all different?
> Whatever my difference, I do not need for it to be tolerated,
> I need my difference to be appreciated and valued.

Our identity is shaped by the culture we are born into, this also influences our internal world and our view of and responses to the external world. We incessantly make judgements and classify others using labels such as gender, class, race, culture, ethnicity, age, religion, sexual orientation, and words such as bigger than and more important than, all used as a way to position ourselves in relation to others. Not only are labels value laden, but they denote difference, power and influence. Labelling is such an intrinsic part of our language, that we are not conscious of its underlying dynamic inter-action. In a society where being White colonises the space of "normal" how conscious are you of being White? If being White is the "norm", what does it make those who are not White? How conscious are you of being White and its impact on your choices and opportunities? How does being White influence your thoughts and behaviour towards others who are not White?

Can you imagine how it might feel when colour and race features in every situation and aspect of your life?

As a Black child I grew up in a wider culture where all that was White was good and anything that was Black was bad and where I was constantly given the message that I was not good enough and that I was second best. Where, at every level of my everyday experi-ence such as at school, the notion of not good enough was often and regularly reinforced in subtle and overt ways. Now an adult, that message is still there, but it is reinforced in a more sophisticated way.

Human beings have an enormous need to belong, to be accepted by peers and/or the group. Perhaps for some of us there were points in our lives, when we felt the need to blend in, be seen as normal and accepted by peers and/or the group. Perhaps our feel-ing of being different stirs up memories of prejudicial, racist and bullying attacks, left over from childhood or experienced as an adult. Our need to belong, to be loved, valued and accepted get played out in our relationships. Perhaps it is through our relation-ships with others and in relating that we learn about ourselves and about acceptance and rejection. This in turn gives us the authority to accept or reject and this becomes internalized and manifests in the rejection or acceptance of different aspects of ourselves, or is played out in our relationships and projected on to others.

In thinking about undertaking a training to become a psycho-therapist, I reconnected with the trauma of the prejudicial and racial attacks I had experienced during childhood and specifically in the educational system that was culturally biased, where I was judged by the colour of my skin and not by my academic ability. Where it was so easy to have become a problem student rather than the problem being recognized as institutional racism projected on to me.

I recognized that in training to become a psychotherapist, I would have to give of myself, take risks, and journey inside where furtively awaits, all the trauma and consequences of oppression—xenophobia, stereotype, prejudice and racism. This raised many questions for me.

I wondered how safe would it be to give of myself? How would giving of myself be received, understood and interpreted? Would my difference be seen, valued and appreciated? Would I be spot lighted? Would I be undermined—my contribution paraphrased? Would I have to justify my presence on the course? Would I have to rationalise my feelings? Would I be subjected to subtle repetitive attacks? Would difference be discussed and if I challenge the normality of being White, how would this be received? Would difference be seen in terms of hierarchy? Would the training consider and accept how differently I might experience the same reality as my fellow students? Would I be expected to be the expert—spokesperson on "Black" issues? Would I have to educate my fellow students about being Black or provide the Black perspective? Would I get the opportunity to explore my own difference and prejudices?

Would the training positively stroke my psyche by providing a racial and cultural perspective along side the White Eurocentric model?

When I became a "Psychotherapist In Training" what was important to me was that, my supervisor would be able to genuinely acknowledge our difference and similarities and be prepared to examine his or her values and attitudes in relation to my difference.

As a psychotherapist, the prospect of a variety of clients means that countless human and social factors are brought into my relationships with my clients which must be explored and understood.

While I do not possess knowledge of all my client's cultures, my starting point is one of respect. The challenge for me is how to apply Western based theory in a range of cultural contexts.

Kareem (1992) argued that a therapeutic approach that does not fully take into account the person's identity, ethnicity, culture and social values would fragment that person.

In working with some clients from a non-British cultural background, I have had to modify the Western psychoanalytic approach.

I have had to look outside of the confines of psychotherapy to understand the significance of the client's perspective and mode of operation to provide understanding and to value where the client is coming from culturally. This would include recognizing their inner experiences and total life experience including communal life experiences in their country of origin, before the therapeutic alliance could be established, which might then give access to their inner world.

In this context, I have found that some basic understanding of the particular client's culture to be essential in reaching an understanding of the range of critical factors, which have contributed to the creation of and maintenance of the client's internal world. This I see as an accumulation of their experiences of and responses to the external world. For example, what is viewed as normal or abnormal, how mental distress is expressed, child rearing patterns, family structures, gender roles, obligations to the community, and the social hierarchy. In addition loss in its many aspects—roots, family, financial issues, social status and life experience in the country of origin. Other factors might include an understanding of the social and political history and construction of the client's society.

Here I want to illustrate what I have been describing by introducing a vignette from my clinical practice.

Mr A, an Eritrean client, was referred for therapy and arrived for our first session with his wife. He introduced them both to me. She seated herself an arm's length away and to his right.

Mr A asked me about my country of origin and how long I had lived in this country? I answered his question.

He explained that he had been told to see me as he was depressed. He did not know what depression was, he did not understand it. In his country when he is sick he goes to the doctor and is made better.

In a small voice he spoke of his past life—running his own company and of being a respected member of his community and head of his family. He spoke of witnessing torture, the disappearance of a younger brother and other family members and of his eventual escape to England.

He spoke of feeling unsafe, of being watched and of the lack of regard shown to him and his wife—they get pushed, people on the estate and on the street tell them that they have no right to be here and to go home. He has nothing, no family of his own, he feels owned, controlled and isolated in a flat on the tenth floor. He questioned his ability to settle in a country where he is different and not accepted, where he is powerless because he doesn't speak the language or understand how things are done. He needed to know who could be trusted.

Ten minutes before the end of our session, Mr A asked whether I had any children and did I not want children. I answered the first part of his question. He said it was a good thing to have children. He shared that he loved children and in his culture children were very important, giving status to the family. He spoke of his wife having undergone fertility treatment and of being assured that they would have up to three attempts. The first attempt at IVF did not result in a pregnancy and on returning for further treatment he was told that there were no more eggs.

I remember feeling Mr A's isolation, despair and resignation, having a sense that he felt cheated and robbed of family life. Their very survival seemed at risk as they could not reproduce.

At the end of the session I reaffirmed the agreed the day and time that would become our regular meeting time. Mr A shook my hand and his wife kissed my cheek.

In preparing to work with Mr A, I enquired as to whether English was his second language and about his skills in English. He was described as having a good command of English having lived here for some three years.

I understood from the initial assessment that Mr A was experiencing depression. I had some awareness of the conflict in Mr A's country where overnight good neighbours and friends had become the enemy within. I was also aware that he had witnessed the torture of family members and friends and had fled his country of origin with his wife and had sought asylum in England where he had no relatives or friends. It was highlighted that his depression was a response to his experience of being tortured, the disappearance of family and friends and now living in a strange country.

From my experience, I had assumed that the therapy sessions with Mr A would be on a one to one basis. I was therefore surprised when he brought his wife to the session as it had not been a couple referral and this would have been outside of my experience of working.

It became clear that before we could enter into a therapeutic relationship Mr A needed to explore and assess our difference and our similarities. I answered his questions as I believe that in the context of his experience back home and currently, he needed to know about me, where I had come from and who I was behind the "blank screen", could he trust me? I understood that some of his anxieties might have included; Would I understand his situation? Could I help him? Would I make it better? Perhaps he might have felt that his very life depended on his assessment of my authenticity—ensuring that I was not a member of the regime from which he had escaped and that I was not someone ready to betray him. I also wondered whether the effects of stereotype, prejudice and racism had begun to impact on Mr A and whether his need to know about me was an expression of internalized oppression?

Having been introduced to Mrs A, I began to wonder how and where she might fit into the therapeutic space and relationship. I was struck by her stillness in the session but yet felt strongly that she was in the room and part of the therapy.

Many questions raced through my mind.

Who is the client?—Are they both clients?—Will Mrs A be present at each therapy session?—What would be her role in the therapy? —Is she here as our interpreter?—What are the sex roles in their culture and family?—Do I include and acknowledge her presence in the session?—If I were to include her, would I need Mr A's permission to do so?—How would I be experienced if I did not include her?

I decided not to seek clarity to my questions and live with the uncertainty, the not knowing, as I felt confident that in time the answers to my questions would unfold.

Throughout the session, Mrs A looked intently at Mr A, who from time to time looked at her and on occasions addressed her directly in their language.

When Mr A spoke with her I felt excluded as I had no way of knowing what was exchanged and I entertained the fantasy that he was checking out the accuracy of his story—seeking clarification or confirmation of an event. Maybe he was checking out her feelings or asking what else he might present on her behalf or perhaps suggesting that I was not good enough.

I connected with Mr A's feelings of alienation, some of which were experienced by my own family when they arrived in England as migrant workers accompanied by the loss of status, loss of respect and of not belonging. Fleeing his country of origin, he experienced the loss of his extended family, the lost opportunity to secure the survival of the family line through IVF—have children and create his own family and to live on through them. Other losses included having to cope with a new order and ways of doing things, perhaps not always understanding how or why. Perhaps the effects of racism and alienation all impacted on Mr & Mr A's internal world, shaping how they see and experience the world and being different. I wondered what Mr A's points of reference were for dealing with his new experiences of being dependent, being stereotyped, suffering oppression, prejudice and racism?

Mr A's hand shake at the end of the session and Mrs A's kiss were an acknowledgement of connectedness and tokens of an alliance and expressions of thanks.

In answer to some of my internal questions about Mrs A's role in the therapeutic space, I believe she was receiving therapy by proxy. Mr A was acting on their behalf in relation to the issues he brought to therapy.

Mr A did not attend the next two arranged sessions. I wrote to him acknowledging the missed appointments and explained that if he still needed our service he should make contact and he would be placed back on the waiting list. Three weeks later, Mr A made contact wanting to be seen that week. I was unable to see him, as I had no available space. He shared with me that back home in Eritrea he would have been seen, as he was well known and respected.

Sadly, my work with Mr and Mrs A ended after only two sessions. I wondered how Mr A's psyche might have been affected by my saying "no" to his request for therapy that week? What impact might my saying "no" have had on his unconscious life?

I wondered if Mr A had been seen by a White therapist would he have had a need to check out their authenticity?

If he needed to check authenticity, how would he have done this?

What kind or type of authenticity would he have needed?

Would he have asked the same questions?

And if he did ask personal questions, how would it have been experienced?

There is a need for open discussion about difference.

As psychotherapists, we are likely to work with a diversity of clients and will be confronted with difference, some of which will be visible, some hidden.

In working with difference there is a need for anti-oppressive practice that operates on the basis of equality and not on dimensions of superiority or inferiority, so that we meet our clients with empathy, respect and positive regard. Perhaps it is only when as a society we learn to accept that difference is not synonymous with "bad" and "dangerous" that difference will be accepted as normal and valued by us and in our future clients.

References

Dupont-Joshua, A. (Ed.) (2003). *Working Inter-Culturally in Counselling Settings*. Hove: Brunner-Routledge.

Kareem, J., & Littlewood, R. (1992). *Intercultural Therapy: Themes, Interpretation and Practices*. Oxford: Blackwell.

Invisibility

Barbara Ashton

When asked to participate in this conference I wondered why me? I read the list of the other speakers and I could see why them but why me, born and bred here in England and lived the majority of my life here? Then, I read the opening paragraph of the flyer.

> Too often issues of race, culture and ethnicity are seen as relevant only to black and ethnic minority psychotherapists and clients. But all psychotherapists and their clients bring a rich diversity of ethnic and cultural narratives to the clinical encounter. Each of us will have a unique and complex sense of who we feel ourselves to be, as well as who others expect us to be, in the ever-shifting contexts of our individual families, societies and cultures. Each of us is likely to grapple with feelings of inclusion and exclusion, belonging and alienation, visibility and invisibility, power and powerlessness.

And the word invisibility leapt out at me. I remembered the second John Bowlby Memorial Conference I attended when Renos Papadopoulos (1999) presented his paper "Storied Community as Secure Base" in response to Nancy Hollander's (1998) paper on "Exile,

Paradoxes of Loss and Creativity". He talked of how people adapt in differing ways to exile and emigration, often within the same family. One person looking forward, seeing only the good, the progress, the cutting off of the past; the other person there in the present but always looking back with a sense of longing. Somehow this felt familiar to me. Later my therapist remarked on the fact that sometimes my responses and feelings around situations were those of an immigrant—she, herself, was not English.

This led to further exploration and I came to realise the impact on my life of the move my working class parents made in 1937 from Oldham, a Lancashire mill town, to Enfield, then a leafy, village-like suburb of London. This move was an economic migration, the promise of work, in a time of depression. For indeed my mother's way of coping with this, and most events, was to say "never look back", "get on with it, inside toilets, a clear sky free from grimy mill smoke". Whilst, with my father, I was always aware of a nostalgia for the past, what was lost and left behind and the pain of where he found himself. Due to the onset of war, in 1939, not a great time to be born, my mother was evacuated to Oldham and I was duly born and lived at my grandparents' house within an extended family, with many of the men absent. Briefly aged two and finally aged four, my parents and I, returned south with all that this entailed; lost, ruptured attachment bonds, and at this time the north/south divide was huge. Exploring the past with my mother in her late eighties, she recalled the time when she got a job in a factory. Her name being Eunice, not a common southern name, and because of her accent, the other women thought she was foreign and so no one spoke to her as they assumed she would not understand what they were talking about. Subsequently I spent many summer holidays with my grandparents, put on the train at Euston by my mother with two shillings for the guard, and met in Manchester by my grandmother. I was aware of these split attachments—a north/south accent and language. Feelings of rootlessness, not really belonging which my brothers, born later in Enfield, never experienced. Thus I realized I was, I am, an INVISIBLE immigrant.

Did this account for my primary adult relationships being with men from other cultures and races? Perhaps this was the reason why so many of my close friends came from different backgrounds. My clinical practice for several years was made up of people from other cultures and even now I have only two English clients. In my past career, teaching, I worked in schools with huge ethnic diversity and felt comfortable there. Finally I realized in therapy how alienated I had felt from the mainstream culture of my own country. It was with joy that I finally realized that the things that I had felt so painfully in the past, the not belonging, now finally, felt exciting and freeing—it can be fun being on the edge.

Is it surprising then that I have been working for the past seven years at ICAP—Immigrant Counselling and Psychotherapy? ICAP was set up in 1997 in order to meet the hugely unmet needs of the Irish population in London, and has grown to encompass other areas with a second centre set up in Birmingham. In fact we have an inclusive referrals policy providing low cost therapy to a wide diversity of people with an emphasis on cultural sensitivity. Quoting from an article in *The Guardian*, a year ago entitled *"When Irish eyes aren't smiling"* (*another stereotype shattered*) ... Herpreet Kaur Grewal writes:

The happy Irishman is sometimes the only way people want to see the Irish community.

Irish people are a virtually INVISIBLE minority within Britain's mental health services, so their suffering tends to be neglected ...

First generation Irish people make up 1.27 per cent of the population—the country's third largest ethnic minority.

According to a new report to be launched in April ... many Irish people say they experience discrimination.

It shows that ... 40 per cent of Irish people within the mental health services rate their experiences negatively ... Irish are more likely to see lack of staff cultural awareness as a problem.

Nearly half reported experiencing racial discrimination linked to cultural insensitivity, stereotyping and exclusion.

The Irish are more likely to be sleeping rough on London streets, 53 per cent more likely to commit suicide. In London Irish people had the highest overall admission rates to hospital compared with black and white populations, especially for depression.

As most Irish people are white they are excluded from the "ethnic minority" agenda. This INVISIBILITY is also responsible for the general lack of interest in Irish health compared with that of other minorities. [Grewal, 2004]

The majority of people coming to ICAP are from this "invisible" population. Often with good reasons for maintaining invisibility in their lives this means they are unable to conceive of a right to be seen or to be heard. Unused to being recognized it can be painful and frightening to enter into therapy, for most an alien concept, and to risk the opening up of old wounds and the possibility of attachment.

In ICAP a number of our clients come with a history of abuse: physical, sexual, institutional and emotional. Many of the survivors have set up and joined support groups, and are involved in commencing action for compensation and recognition. Thus this invisible minority have begun to recall and tell their stories. Due to funding received from the Irish Government, ICAP is able to offer open ended therapy and works creatively in order to hold and contain people until the therapy space is safe enough to enter.

This can take a long time and whilst boundaries are kept, the therapeutic framework needs to be creative. I am reminded of the child with chaotic attachment patterns who in the strange situation test will move towards the adult and suddenly freeze—this is often how it feels in the first months . . . sometimes a call, "I am half way there but can't make it, I've hit a wall". Absences, especially around breaks, letters and phone calls and what all this means, "I wait to see if a letter will arrive, to see if you are to be trusted, are sticking by me". The moving time when suddenly, for some people for the first time, a realization of attachment and what it means. The understanding that somebody cares whether or not you are there.

At present our premises are adjoining a large Catholic church and this raises issues for some people, in particular the survivors of institutional abuse; is ICAP linked to the church and funded by them? Since the church is such a large part of Irish culture, it opens the door to the question; what does it mean to one's spirituality when this is where the abuse originated? Other questions raised include: How does it feel to be Irish, when your own country offered you no protection to then come to another country which does not offer respect or sanctuary? Is this a common experience for many immigrants?

Within this client population there is often a third person in the room—the ongoing claim for compensation which involves legal proceedings or psychiatric reports. It is moving and horrifying to sit with someone who once again has been re-traumatized by having to tell his or her story in front of a stranger, in one sitting. Unravelling my anger, frustration and pain following these sessions, from my client's inability to express or think that this is not right, is difficult.

Learning to become invisible at an early age in order to escape physical or sexual abuse, hopefully; being told and made to realize that indeed you were "nothing", and had no right to be born, witnessing the fact that children were nothing—leaves a legacy of expecting nothing for oneself. Much of the work is around discovering a voice and a sense of self. I am working with people aged between their early 30's and 70, some of whom were institutionalized as babies. After years of work it is wonderful when I hear how someone stood up at a meeting and found his or her voice. It is interesting how women cannot find a voice initially for themselves but can find it for their children, or grandchildren; and later to be witness to a woman's voice which has become loud, disconcerting, not easy to listen to . . . a voice of protest. I long to shout "Oh yes!!!" For in the past this loud protesting voice would have been so dangerous.

Of course with the attachment comes fear and absences. Also disappointment, . . . the disappointment of the boundaries and limitations of therapy. I cannot go to Ireland as a companion and witness in the hearings despite the fact I am the one who knows the story. Coming to terms with this can be a crucial point in the therapy, surviving the anger and rage. My own feelings of inadequacy at this time—I recall Winnicott, the mother who must be destroyed in order to be internalized. When I hear "but you will be here when I get back" that is a "now" moment (Stern, 1998).

I quote from a paper by Tamar Shoshan (1989), writing on the Holocaust, entitled "Mourning and Longing from Generation to Generation":

Violent sudden separation from their closest family members determined the extent of survivors' individual traumas.

Countless hours of in-depth interviews with dozens of Holocaust survivors demonstrate, almost without exception that the experience of being violently and totally torn from close family stands at the centre of the survivors' trauma. The moments of sudden and final separation are forever imprinted deep in their souls . . .

Although they underwent many dreadful experiences both before and after the separation, it was at that point that they began to become anonymous, without identity utterly alone, detached. [Shoshun, 1989, p. 193–207]

This feels so relevant to the adult survivors I work with. The initial tearing away from, or loss of, the primary attachment figure, always the mother in my experience, seems to overshadow all the trauma that follows and is a central part of the therapeutic work. It takes differing forms. A loss and being left with absolutely nothing; no knowledge of family or background; the constant search for this, with the help of others, but no feeling of a right to this knowledge for oneself. The searching for the lost mother.

In some cases the reconciliation with caregiver, only to be rejected. The shattering of the fantasies and expectations of what it was hoped it would be like. Thus, alongside the abuse, going out into the world with no preparation; often leading women into abusive relationships and dangerous situations. Indeed, then working with the second generation, children of these women.

What do we see? What do we think? What do we feel?

A multitude of all things—both my clients and myself see so many things. Sometimes the issues of racism and culture are in the room, particularly with reference to a colonized people and power. Also language is significant, I have to remember that for many people, historically, English is their second language. I have been privileged to learn so much about Irishness, both from clients and from ICAP, indeed from all sides. At times it is assumed I am Irish . . . "couldn't get on with the other therapist, she was so English". Decisions about when to disclose my own background, when not to, it is all a part of the work. At times admitting a lack of understanding, asking for knowledge and then at other times these issues are not in the room at all.

In 2000 I was asked to write a brief comment on my work at ICAP for their annual report, this is what I wrote and I realize it still expresses how I feel about my work:

One of the things that personally makes my work here especially rewarding is the variety of people using the Centre. My experience includes both men and women, homosexual, heterosexual, single and partnered, mothers, fathers and grandparents, ranging in age from early twenties to late sixties . . . a mixture of cultures, Irish, Italian, Turkish, Australian, Nigerian, Ugandan and Afro-Caribbean. The basis for my work is, quoting Barbara Fletchman Smith (2000), author of *Mental Slavery*, "people are first and foremost, individuals". [Ashton, 2000]

References

Ashton, B. (2000). Immigrant Counselling and Psychotherapy, Annual Report, 2000.

Fletchman Smith, B. (2000). *Mental Slavery: Psychoanalytic Studies of Caribbean People*. London: Rebus Press.

Grewal, H. K. (2004). When Irish eyes aren't smiling. *The Guardian*: Society Section. ll. 2ff.

Hollander, N. (1998). Exile: Paradoxes of Loss and Creativity. John Bowlby Memorial Lecture. *British Journal of Psychotherapy*, 2: 201–215.

Papadopoulos, R. (1999). Storied Community as Secure Base. A response to Nancy Hollander, Exile: Paradoxes of Loss and Creativity. John Bowlby Memorial Leccture. *British Journal of Psychotherapy*, 3: 322–332.

Shoshan, T. (1989). Mourning and longing from generation to generation. *American Journal of Psychotherapy*, 43(2), 193–207.

Stern, D., & The Process of Change Study Group (1998). Non-interpretive mechanisms in psychoanalytic psychotherapy: the "something more" than interpretation. *International Journal of Psycho-Analysis, 79*: 903–921.

Unmasking difference, culture, and attachment in the psychoanalytic space

"Don't you make my blue eyes brown"

Irris Singer

Myself

I would like to set the scene by saying something about my family background and how it relates to my own sense of difference. I have a photograph of two of my grandchildren, one so fair, and one so dark, which reflects my core experience of difference. These two beautiful little boys are an embodiment of my parents' (their great-grandparents) colour differences and how they were in the world. And of course, my parents' colour codedness deeply impacted on my sense of self and how I am in the world. Even so, my parents' individual difference was in fact only one component of difference in my childhood; they were part of my extended Yiddish speaking immigrant family which located itself in a very small, very English village during World War 2. The women folk, our grandmother, mothers and aunts, protected themselves and the children from the safety of our cottage, and were no doubt conspicuous by their absence in village life, while the men folk, our grandfather, fathers and uncles stayed in London visiting us in their long coats and trilby hats late Saturday night and leaving before the first light on Monday morning. I remember the adult sense of foreboding, conveyed in hushed Yiddish, which lurked beneath our childhood fun of shared tin baths, shared beds, storytelling, all submerged in the clouds of steam and smells of our mothers' endless washing and cooking. Sometimes we children played with the village children on the ruins of a house which a stray German bomb had destroyed, but we were not allowed to visit the children in their homes. One kind neighbour "Uncle Frank" brought us a small Christmas tree each year, which our bewildered mothers did not like to refuse, even though the word itself, Christmas, was forbidden in our family. The tree stood forlornly unadorned in a corner of the living room, avoided by the adult eyes, while we children secretly longed to decorate it. Some years later, after the war when I was eight years old, my father came to my bed late at night to tell me that the United Nations had voted in favour of a homeland for the Jews, the State of Israel. Poland was no longer *de haeme* (the "homeland") and apparently neither was England. It appeared that Israel was now our home and we would be going there as soon as possible. We were no longer to be strangers in a strange land.

These are the experiences that have influenced my standing here today talking about difference.

Psychotherapists and difference

I have led many workshops and seminars with psychotherapists exploring the feelings and awareness of our own difference, and the difference of the other sitting with us in the therapy space. In small groups participants first share their experiences and feelings of their own difference, and then experiences and feelings of the other's difference. The words below are a sample of the words and feelings that therapists have most commonly used to describe their own and the other's, difference.

Me as Different . . .

I felt . . . misunderstood . . . shocked . . . frustrated . . . cast out . . . rejected . . . excluded . . . isolated . . . alone . . . lonely . . . vulnerable . . . skinless . . . invisible . . . deadened . . . inferior . . .

I became ... searching ... singled out ... exposed ... special ... exotic ... proud ... empowered ... superior ...

I experienced ... fluctuating self-esteem ... confusion ... shame ... anger ...

I felt ... damaged ... bitter ... stunted ... delinquent ... deviant ...

I became ... a keen reader ... pseudo-independent ... needy-but-defiant ... political ... rebellious ... doubtful-of-my-sanity ... rejecting ... militant ... in a double bind ...

When different, I am ... fragile ... strong ... sad ... hurt.

The Other as Different ...

I can't deal with difference ... I deny difference and act as if not denying it ... I am not acknowledging it ...

I experience ... anxiety and inability to think ... loss of civility ... killing off the different other with language ... anger ... resentment ... negativity ... want to destroy it ... hate.

I hate ... being apart from ... being shut out ... attack on sense of self ... loss of my self ... aloneness.

Over compensation ... I wish I was like that ... idealization. ... transference ... envy.

Poles of love and hate ... oscillating ... idealization/denigration ... value judgements ... thank god you're different ... wanting some-one to act as I do ... to change me ... ambivalence.

I feel ... compassion ... similarity ... testing the relationship ... what is real? I am mourning what could have been ... what I am not ... resigned.

These words express the powerful emotions that are present and ongoing throughout our lives, in every intra- and inter-relational encounter, private or public, conscious or unconscious, underlying our perceptions of one another. They are relevant to my presentation today which is about how two groups of "other", two groups of "enemies" negotiate their perceptions of the other.

The Bereaved Parents' Circle

Moving out from Cascia Davis' and Barbara Ashton's sensitive work (in this volume) about difference in the therapy space, I am applying a similar psychoanalytic critique of difference in a socio-political space.

I begin with a description of a film clip from The Bereaved Parents' Circle. They are a group of Palestinian and Israeli families, whose children have been killed by the other side. These bereaved parents, in the context of a brutalizing occupation and resistance, are struggling to unmask their differences.

The Bereaved Parents' Circle (BPC) began in 1996 when a distraught bereaved Israeli father made contact with another bereaved father. Their loss was so great, overriding all political considerations that they invited all bereaved parents in the conflict, Israeli and Palestinian, to join them in an effort to persuade the government to stop killing children. Today the group, The Bereaved Parents' Circle and Family Forum number around 500 families in almost equal numbers from both sides. The BPC has several important functions. One is of sharing mourning through listening and telling one another their stories. Some speak of the Circle being their new and only real family. Some members are deeply committed peace activists. In Israeli-Palestinian pairs they visit schools and community centres in Israel and Palestine, and tour abroad working for peace through the powerful message of the death of their loved ones "stop killing the children". Their belief in dialogue has been extended to a free open telephone service between Israel and Palestine with thousands of contacts made every week.

I am asking . . .

- What characterizes these parents, that enables them to seek co-existence and life rather than revenge and death?
- "What is going on" in the Bereaved Parents' Circle that facilitates fraternity rather than revenge?

- What might we learn from them that can be applied in other conflict ridden areas?
- What might we learn from them that we can take back into the therapy space?

The film "Tears of Peace" was made in 2000 to illustrate the work of the BPC (Buchman, 2000). It focuses on two fathers, Yehuda, an Israeli, and Ramadan, a Palestinian, whose stories are followed in this film and who touch the viewer with their common humanity and authenticity. They are similar physically and in dress; both have an unassuming manner and direct, but low key, way of telling their story. We see them struggle with their painful memories and their desire to communicate to us as simply as possible the trauma of their sons' deaths. The mothers don't appear, except Selma Zaidan, a Druze mother, who has lost two sons and a brother.

The film opens with a video of a young, frightened, Israeli soldier, hands tied behind him seated in front of an Arab soldier strapped with bullets, his face and head hidden by a kafiya, with only his eyes visible. (The kafiya is the traditional black and white headscarf, symbol of the of Palestinian Liberation Organization.)

Holding up the Israeli soldier's identity card the Arab soldier says in Arabic "We Az-Adin El Kasam, the armed section of Hamas, are responsible for the abduction of Nahshon Vaksman". Nahshon's eyes move hopelessly downwards. He says, in Hebrew, "I am asking you to do what you can to get me out alive". The Arab soldier drops his hand with the ID card, and lowers his head and eyes while Nahshon speaks. (I am reminded of Wilfred Owen's (1918) First World War poem "Strange Meeting").

The date is 14.9.94 and the heading *Prayer for Nahshon* comes up as the camera moves to the centre of Jewish prayer, the Wailing Wall. We see religious Jews in prayer for Nahshon and then a close up of Nahshon's father, Yehuda, on screen. He is a homely looking bearded man wearing a work day blue check shirt, a sweater, and a religious skull cap. He speaks slowly and his voice thickens. "The helplessness almost drove me crazy. You can go crazy from stress, fear and worry. If only I had been there instead of him."

The camera moves across hills to the Arab village of Bir Naballa which is two and a half metres away from where the Vaksmans live. Yehuda continues with great pain, "They told us that he was in

Gaza. It would have taken me only a few minutes to get to him" (to Bir Naballa, where Nahshon was actually held).

We see Yehuda praying in a local synagogue still dressed in his check shirt and sweater and then we are in a Mosque where Ramadan Azam is praying; the two men are similar in age, attire and appearance. The scene moves into Ramadan's workshop above his house. Like Yehuda, he speaks slowly. "It was ten years ago, my son lived here with me. We lived here and worked upstairs. I said to Ahmad, *Ahmad, take money and go get me some cement*. He took the cart and the horse and after an hour in the Kasam mosque nearby I suddenly heard shots." We see street scenes in Gaza of Israeli soldiers shooting in the streets and people running in all directions. Ramadan continues in a reflective non-dramatic voice, his eyes engaging ours. "A friend came over, he knew my son had been killed. He said to me, *Ramadan, how do you feel?* I said OK. He said to me, *where is your son?* I said, *he went to get cement.* He said, *are you sure?* I said, *yes.* He said, *are you a man?* I said, *yes, yes, what happened?* So I said to him, *has Ahmad been killed?* and he said, *no.* I said to him, *speak, has Ahmad been killed?* and he said, *yes, yes.*"

The camera cuts to Ramadan and his two teenage sons praying over Ahmad's grave in a quite unattended Palestinian cemetery, then moves over to a Jewish cemetery and Nahshon's grave.

Again there is a close up of Yehuda's face "I wanted to avenge him, but I came to the conclusion that to murder Palestinians, or to send someone else to murder Palestinians, won't help. What will it give me? It won't return my son to me. It will cause them to counter revenge me, and there will be no end to revenge. I decided to enter into the shoes of the other side, and to see the conflict, not only from the Israeli side, but also from the Palestinian side. (Images come on screen of deserted and destroyed houses and streets in Gaza.) I came to the conclusion that there is a reason for their complaints. Their anger is valid. So I decided to participate in the activities of the Bereaved Parents' Circle and to travel to Gaza with the bereaved parents. (Scenes of Israeli and Palestinian members talking together at a meeting.) These meetings aim to create a group who will support the peace process."

The film moves to a meeting of the Bereaved Parents' Circle. The founder member Yizhak Frankental is talking to the meeting; "The pain is shared. We not only share the same piece of land, but we also share what is lying below it, the graves of our children." A bereaved Druze Palestinian mother, Selma Zaidan stands and continues, "We paid a dear and heavy price. (She breathes deeply as she controls her tears). I paid with two sons and a brother. No war in the world is worth this price." (Close ups of other bereaved parents at the meeting listening, sad and tearful.)

Ramadan then addresses the meeting—"Ahmad, may he rest in peace, was a good boy. He gave all that he had for his parents; he loved his family, his brothers and sisters. He loved them dearly." (We see Ahmad's grandparents silently crying, and wiping away tears.)

Yehuda Vaksman, smiling in memory says ". . . I remember when he was four years old," (we see Ramadan and Selma's attentive and pained faces), "I'd hug him . . . for half a minute . . . and he'd say, Daddy, just a little more, just a little more . . ."

The film zooms in on two memorial candles in close up, one with the inscription "in memory of Palestinian victims", and the other "in memory of Israeli victims".

The final scenes are close ups of Ramadan and Yehuda. Ramadan says, "Just like I lost my son, the Jew has lost his son, or daughter. There is no difference between us. Just like I'm a father, so is he."

Yehuda, in his slow and painfully honest voice says, "If parents who have lost their children are able to sit together and talk about better days to come in the future, those who haven't suffered so much, all the more so."

Ramadan and Yehuda clasp hands and embrace.

Theoretical framework

I am always hugely moved by this film, and by this group. It is hard to critique other peoples' pain. There is something both super luminary and subliminal about such extreme experiences of death and pain that almost defies critique and understanding. I find myself bewildered by the complexity of difference that becomes apparent in the Bereaved Parents' Circle. A complexity made up of a configuration of many overlapping Venn diagrams of commonality within the difference.

I have tried to identify tensions, within that complexity that are being held by this group, through the lens of Western psychoanalytic theory. I acknowledge the distortions that arise when applying Western psychoanalytic concepts to non-Western cultures. Aware that we lack the benefit of action-based enquiry, my questions nevertheless stem from a relational theoretical framework.

We can begin by looking at mourning and trauma. Infant and child death in third world countries is not uncommon and the Middle East has well tried cultural and religious mourning processes. But in what ways do they answer the needs of a society caught up in psycho-social trauma? All of the parents we meet in the film are religious, but their mourning process reaches beyond the religious rituals. Sharing the mourning in this context seems easier than private personal mourning. Jo Berry, of the Forgiveness Project, whose father, a conservative MP, was killed in an IRA bomb attack at a political party conference, speaks of the aloneness of victims rebuilding life after death. She points out that perpetrators, religious leaders and governments are keen to move on from the trauma. There are few institutionalized mourning processes for the survivors.

Telling the story and having it witnessed is a therapy practice we have learnt from many cultures and is endorsed by dialoguing groups. This process may alleviate the pain of a death they see as senseless, expressed in the anguish of the words "my son died for nothing". Hearing one another's stories may help to make some sense, in the senselessness of their own child's death.

The fathers in the film talk of their helplessness in the face of the traumatic death of their children, reminiscent of the experience of some Holocaust survivors whose helplessness was often transmitted as far as third generation survivors. Despite their helplessness, the BPC parents have engaged in a process of regaining a sense of agency. They are empowered by their project to bring their message of "stop killing the children" to schools and community venues within Israel, Palestine and to the wider world.

The parents in the film, Yehuda, Ramadan, Selma, Yizhak, and indeed all the BPC parents, are living in the social breakdown and chaos found in psycho-social trauma. In addition they have experienced the trauma of one or more of their children's or other family member's violent, and sometimes sadistic deaths in the service of their governments' policies. The effects and symptoms of trauma are well documented, as are the defences of disassociation and denial. In addition the parents must cope with changing government policies toward killing and death. They are caught between policies encouraging revenge killings and policies of halting killings during periods of reconciliation. Death is sometimes heroic and sometimes sidelined. In the film all the parents blame their governments for the death of their children, and call on citizens to seek a bottom-up people solution in protest against government policies, to "stop the killing of children". It is a contradiction to expect governments to institutionalise processes for mourning at the same time as following policies of violent, sadistic and pointless death. Through their life affirming action, the BPC parents have found an organic and spontaneous processing of their mourning, which is also a learning experience of how to cope with grief.

Indeed, few countries in conflict have engaged with institutionalized processes for dialogue, mourning and reconciliation, besides government amnesty policies. Members of the Forgiveness Project speak of how forgiveness may well victimise the survivors by asking them to give up hate, anger, and pain, and indeed serve the perpetrators' need to move on, before the trauma has been psychologically processed. In addition, all this may be felt by the family as a betrayal of the loved one who died. The Bereaved Parents' involvement in their peace work with the "enemy" seems to have precisely the opposite effect. Rather than betraying the loved one who died they are preserving and keeping the child alive, particularly where the child sought peace and co-existence, as with Yitzhak Frankental's son. One mother told me that parenting is also kept alive.

Attachment theory within chaos and trauma

The members of the Bereaved Parents' Circle are exploring alternatives. Without a secure base there is no exploration. There has to be a secure enough setting in which to unmask and explore difference. What can we learn about the nature of the base that these parents have created in the Circle, within their grossly chaotic and traumatic environment? As one mother said, reminding me of Winnicott's

(1989) essay "Fear of Breakdown", "Those who can't travel to the other side are victims of fear, the worst has already happened." As in insecure attachment and its associated behaviour, she explained that "victims of fear", fear the physical and the emotional journey to the other side. But Yehuda says, *before* he was a member of the BPC "I decided to put myself in the shoes of the other side". Is this true for all the bereaved parents who took that first step to visit the BPC? What of bereaved parents who were invited to join the BPC but refused? We do not have their story.

Yehuda and Ramadan reject revenge because "it would not help, would not return my son to me". Holding the tension between the past and the future, members of the BPC have prioritized the future, as opposed to other groups who are committed to revenge, prioritizing death and the past, and loss of the future.

The BPC's emphasis on the future, and the peace work they have undertaken is about ensuring life for children in the future, and paradoxically keeps the lost child alive and so parenting too, continues. The child did not die in vain.

My question is what can we learn from the bereaved parents who are able to make that journey? What might we learn from their early internalized experiences, and self-other representations that have supported them during the trauma and chaos? What part might attachment patterns have played in their decision to put themselves in the shoes of the other side? Is the ability to create a "secure base" (Bowlby (1988: 11), in the Circle an outgrowth of the individuals' secure base, or of some other experience? How would we go about exploring that?

The task of unmasking the other, from a secure base, has been illuminated for us by Jessica Benjamin's theories on intersubjectivity (Benjamin, 1995).

The following diagrams are my diagrammatic representations of Benjamin's description of the intersubjective search for the real other, as opposed to our creation of the other through the intrapsychic lens.

The first diagram (1) entitled *Intrapsychic Closed System*, traces Benjamin's description of our search for recognition by the other, essential for our sense of self. To achieve this we need to reach beyond our intra-psychic projections onto the other. Those projections create a demonized or idealized object who will never be able to give us real recognition.

(1) Intrapsychic Closed System

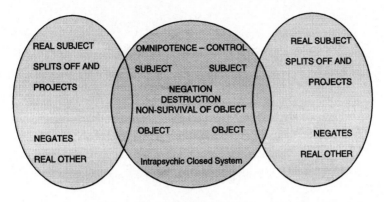

The second diagram (2) entitled *Survival and Recognition* and the third (3) called *Recognition and Alterity*, represent the process of how we must retrieve our projections in order to recognise the other as a real subject who can then reciprocally recognise us. Benjamin describes the to-ing and fro-ing between the object created by our projections, and the real other as subject, as a violent, life long intra-psychic struggle involving the intensity of both love and hatred.

(2) Survival and Recognition

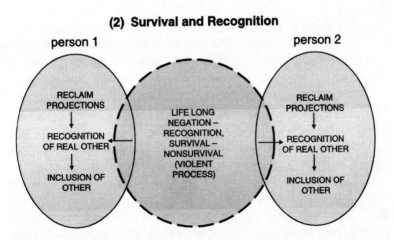

Some of the parents in the film are still involved in that struggle, Yitzhak Frankental says in a later film that if he finds his son's murderers he will kill them while in contrast a mother, in London, said

(3) Recognition and Alterity

I		OTHER
RECLAIM PROJECTIONS		A REAL, NOT-PROJECTED OTHER
DIFFERENT	SAME	DIFFERENT
WE SURVIVED NEGATION, SEPARATION & ALTERITY		WE EXIST BY & THROUGH MUTUAL RECOGNITION
WE CAN SHARE AND FEELINGS		THOUGHTS FROM ALTERITY
YOU ARE OUTSIDE		MY INTRAPSYCHIC SPACE

her search is for justice, completion and understanding. In the film we see that projections onto the "enemy", even the murderer, are at least temporarily retrieved, and there is found a human other, similar, but different, from themselves.

The parents appear to have retrieved their projections onto the other's ethnic, cultural, religious, or political identities revealing the real other, and an underlying commonality wherein lies, paradoxically, our true differences. I wonder about the interface and the prioritizing between the process of unmasking the other, and in this case rehumanizing the enemy, while dealing with death and mourning. I heard a mother say, comforted by the concept of dehumanization—"they didn't kill my son, they didn't know him, it was the work of dehumanization". Violence is about losing humanity. The perpetrator of violence is also a victim of violence. Perhaps the strongest tension being held in the group is that of the perpetrator and the victim within us all. In a later film one mother says "did my son kill hers?" but leaves unspoken, did her son kill mine?

Jo Berry, in a public meeting of the Forgiveness Project, said she wanted to know why someone had to kill her father in order to have their voice heard. She said she must keep her heart open. How do we understand psychoanalytically "keeping our heart open"? Is that about retrieving the projections and connecting with the real other?

We cannot look at the individual or the group without taking into account the impact of the socio-political context. Power hierarchies of oppression in race, gender, sexual preference, ability, class and age, are played out in all relationships, in groups and in therapy. How does the Circle manage to exist within the external political reality and maintain their own internal agenda and integrity? How is the imbalance of power between Israelis and Palestinians experienced in the Bereaved Parents' Circle as they struggle to rehumanize the enemy? Perhaps it all adds up to the *fraternity* that Stan Cohen (2001) identifies in his book, *States of Denial*; this, he concludes, will be our ultimate protection against Human Rights' abuses.

How are external socio-political hierarchies, oppressions and practices reflected within the group? The film director, with a loving eye, has carefully balanced the time and attention afforded to Israeli and Palestinian members, and to their environment. However the language of the film is Hebrew. The notices are in Hebrew. The majority of the film crew are Israeli. When there isn't a film director to balance the imbalance of power, with its attendant envy and guilt, how does it impact on the two different groups? Both Palestinian and Israeli parents have told me that their families and friends are angry with them, because they feel the death of their loved one has been cheapened by this relationship with the murderous enemy. While some bereaved parents have managed to change their narrative, others have not, sometimes resulting in family break up.

The action-based researcher is not a blank screen. I have my own agenda, with my own projections, transference and counter transference to the Bereaved Parents' Circle, the Palestinian and the Israeli agenda. I am an Israeli, with a home and children and grandchildren in Israel Palestine, a mother and grandmother who also wants the killing to stop, supports co-existence and would like to spread the inspired BPC message into other areas of conflict.

I believe those aims will best be met by pursuing the approach of action-based research that will facilitate the journeys of all who are inspired by and concerned with the BPC project, from within and without, to interact, question and learn from one another.

Thanks to Daniel Wade and Caroline Parker for their assistance in drawing the diagrams for this chapter.

References

Baskin, G. (2000). *Bottom-Up. Creating Peace from the Bottom-Up*. Israel: IPCRI (http://www.ipcri.org/files/bottom-up.html).

Benjamin, J. (1995). *Like Subjects, Love Objects*. New Haven: Yale University Press.

Bowlby, J. (1988). *A Secure Base: Clinical Applications of Attachment Theory*. London: Routledge.

Buchman, S. (2000). *Tears of Peace*. Editor, Aye Huberman, written, directed and produced by Sigal Buchman. All copy rights with The Beareaved Parents' Circle.

Cohen, S. (2001). *States of Denial*. Cambridge: Polity Press.

Fonagy, P. (2001). *Attachment Theory and Psychoanalysis*. New York: Other Press.

Holmes, J. (1993). *John Bowlby and Attachment Theory*. London: Routledge.

Manenti, A. (1999). *Psychosocial Trauma as Inhumanization*. WHO: Regional Office for Europe. Partnership in Health and Emergency Assistance.

Owen, W. (1921). *Poems*. London: Chatto and Windus.

Singer, I. (2002). *A Culture of Peace, an Explosive Concept. An Attachment Perspective*. Conference paper for International Forum for the Culture of Peace.

Winnicott, D. W. (1989). Fear of Breakdown. In: C. Winnicott, R. Shepherd, & M. Davis (Eds), *Psychoanalytical Explorations*, 87–95. London: Karnac.

The John Bowlby Memorial Lecture 2005

How race is lived in the consulting room

Kimberlyn Leary

Introduction

Whenever one writes a paper—and however long it remains in circulation—it belongs, in some sense, to the time and place of its origin. This paper is no exception. Written during the summer of 2001, it is essentially a reflection on race and racial reasoning before the cataclysm of September 11th. For many Americans, especially those culturally accustomed to thinking of themselves as individuals alone, one of the continuing legacies of September 11th is the frightening awareness that one could be targeted simply because one is a member of a group. For many other Americans, immigrants and others, such awareness is a self-conscious fact they have lived with for a very long time.

In the intervening years since September 11th, the face of race in America has almost literally been transformed. Racial reasoning continues to include the familiar declension into "us vs. them" even as those accepted as "us" reflect new alliances. We need look no further than one headline from *New York Times*: "9/11 Bridged the Racial Divide, New Yorkers say gingerly" (*New York Times*, June 16, 2002). In the article, Dean Murphy and David Halbfinger suggest that a growing number of New Yorkers say that they are witnessing a change in race relations since the terrorist attacks. The shift in racial attitudes, noticed in the days and weeks following September 11th but enduring since then, has been manifest in an increased rapprochement between blacks and whites and a lessened tendency to "overreact" [sic] to perceived injustices. By contrast, the dynamics of prejudice and defensive exclusion now extend most openly to South Asians, to people from Middle Eastern backgrounds, to those who are Muslim. This, sadly, has become the psychology of the "new normal".

The forces underlying this shift are readily apparent. Kevin Pough, a 41-year-old, African-American, quoted in Murphy and Halbfinger (2002), nicely sums up psychoanalytic theories of splitting and projection:

> Maybe it's just an illusion I'm having, but when I talk to people, they're not looking at me as a black person anymore . . . Now we are singling out the Arabs . . . Sometimes I think it's like how many faces do we wear? When all this goes all the way, when we put the terrorists away, are we going to go back to the way we were before?

And so, this paper written before September 11th addresses most specifically as its topic this "way we were before". I think, however, that we all appreciate that this way we were before is this way we are still now. The projections at the core of racism, ethnocentrism and the homophobias are fragile, illusory solutions to the psychic challenge difference may pose. The need for effective thinking about race and useful collaborations with respect to diversity is a need made all the more urgent in the post-September 11th milieu that is our world. I hope that some of the thoughts that follow may serve as a stimulus to those efforts.

How Race is Lived in America

The title of this paper "How Race is Lived in the Consulting Room" was designed to invoke another set of headlines from the New York Times—"How Race is Lived in America"—a special series which ran on the front pages of the Times during the summer of 2000 and which was recently released as a book (Lelyveld 2001). Examining public and private conversation about race relations, the editors concluded that most Americans define race less by political action and more by their "daily experience in schools, in sports arenas, pop culture, at worship and in the work place". Critically acclaimed for its comprehensive focus, it is interesting to note that not one of the fifteen articles looked into the issue of race relations in primary heath care or in the provision of mental health services. My intention is to speak to just this gap and suggest that psychoanalysis may offer an important if also paradoxical voice in what is an interdisciplinary effort to put a finger to the pulse of race in American cultural life.

This then is this context in which I will look at race and racial difference in the psychoanalytic consulting room. My frame is as follows. I begin with the assumption that race and ethnicity inflect clinical process, subtly and explicitly. Secondly, I believe that contemporary analytic formulations (e.g. enactment and clinical intersubjectivity) as well as multicultural perspectives outside of psychoanalysis are required if we are to define new sites for psychologically relevant and emotionally meaningful understandings of race.

Now for some, the very notion of psychoanalysis and multi-culturalism in the same sentence might inspire cynicism. This is a scepticism I can appreciate. The biases of classical psychoanalysis—its assumption of universality and heterosexual privilege—are well known. At the same time, clinical psychoanalysis has undergone something of a radical transformation during the last twenty-five years. Psychoanalysis is now actively grappling with the fact that in good treatments their patients almost always extract something considerably beyond the pure insight and self-understanding that theory dictated was the goal of an analytic treatment (Friedman, 2000).

Postmodern and feminist critiques have ushered in even more decisive changes as psychoanalytic theories of development and clinical change have shifted to accommodate a view of truth that is co-constructed and intersubjectively located. Rather than being a blank screen or "analyzing instrument", the analyst is understood to be a quite real counterforce against whom the patient continually bumps. The analytic work therefore consists of giving their differing subjectivities an articulated voice. A focus on analytic interaction and the ubiquity of enactments have, in turn, generated new ways of speaking to the complexity of clinical transactions, including as they relate to race and ethnicity. The result is that psychoanalysis has begun to think more comprehensively about cultural difference and to recognize itself as a culture, and a minority culture one at that.

I'd like to develop several themes that I have been exploring in some of my recent work. They include: (1) What is gained and lost when racial material is viewed as a psychoanalytic expression of personal psychology; (2) the challenges of dealing with racialized subjectivity in clinical treatment; and (3) a discussion of the way in which race illuminates tensions in our contemporary constructs of self and identity. To do so, I'm going to refer to clinical vignettes drawn from my own analytic practice as well as from published case reports in the analytic literature.

As I've indicated, psychoanalysis has had a curious relationship to issues of race and culture. On the one side, psychodynamic models are based almost entirely on the pathologies and protections of the Western nuclear family. Psychoanalysis is cut from the very fabric of culture. Yet until very recently, psychoanalysts assumed that the psychology of those who were white, male and economically well-off was universally applicable to all. Such a view carefully preserves the status quo. Vestiges of this way of thinking creep into our nomenclature today. Consider the common designation the "culturally different patient". What we decide is "different" is, of course, only that which is distinguishable when compared to the majority. A judgment of "difference" is always relative to some criterion that is then implicitly or covertly normed as being healthy or proper.

Clinical illustration one

William, a white man in a four times weekly psychoanalysis with me, sought treatment to deal with what he termed his inhibitions and what he dubbed as his "self-induced hesitations." For most of his life, William has been unable to shake the irksome idea that he has been in some vague way cheated from his due and he struggles with his aggressive resentment over this state of affairs. Keeping quiet about his ambitions and interests has seemed to William to be his best hope for fulfilling them on some future if also far off occasion. Much of his analysis has been directed towards understanding the fantasies underlying his hesitations and deferrals. These include William's expectation that all people are self-involved and rigidly demanding, requiring William's accommodation if he is to secure even the most minimal of comforts. William and I have also explored the ways in which some of his experience of others resonates with his experience of himself. William identifies with demanding others, wanting to control the people in his life as keenly as he feels they control him.

Resuming his analytic sessions after a short break occasioned by my being out of town, William reports a dream that he had in my absence. He dreamed of a boat with a black keel. Somehow the keel got detached and the boat couldn't go anywhere.

William and I discuss his dream. He readily identifies himself with the boat. It is a powerful and imposing piece of machinery. This is an image he would like to have of himself. He had a hard time concentrating on work last Friday (the day of the missed session). He missed me.

I know that although William has been in analysis for several years, he is only now growing comfortable with the psychological intimacy of the consulting room. William went on to say that it is the keel that keeps the boat afloat. When he doesn't comment on the keel being black, I ask about it. It is interesting, he thinks, that he said that the keel was black. The keel on his boat is white but the keel in his dream was distinctly black. William doesn't need me to suggest that the black keel has something to do with me. "You're like my keel," he says quietly. "But last week," I reply, "I left you beached." For the remainder of the session, we explore the ways in which William had felt bereft and angry at his inability to control my comings and goings away but did not feel entitled to complain.

William's transference equation of his absent African-American analyst with the missing black keel is an example of what Kris Yi (1998) has referred to as a "race based transference". In this sense; William's dream is not "about" race *per se*. William makes use of his analyst's blackness idiosyncratically in order to organize his relational experience with his analyst. Race becomes a therapeutically available surface on which William is able to convey his transference hopes and dreads.

My question is this: how complete is this understanding of William's psychology? Everyday analytic perspectives like these frame racial experience in psychotherapy largely in terms of the patient's psychology. This can obscure any involvement that the analyst may have in the unfolding of treatment events even though it is the racial difference between analyst and patient that results in the transference being, if you will, "colorized", in the first place (Yi, 1999).

I believe that there are certain unintended problems that follow when psychoanalysts theorize race in this everyday way. For example, the analyst's (or the patient's) race is treated as something of an encrypted code to be deciphered into its underlying psychoanalytic meanings (Leary, 1997). Race is implicitly theorized as being only "skin deep" and its importance as an independent aspect of personal social identity is de-emphasized (Leary, 1997). Further, formulations like these tend to treat race and ethnicity as pertaining only to people of color, rather than as dynamic constellations with relevance to all persons (Leary, 1995).

Clinical illustration two

The psychology of the consulting room becomes considerably more complex in the following exchange. In a later session, William tensely reports that he had breakfast at a new restaurant in Detroit that is owned by the singer Anita Baker. William remembered the controversy surrounding the renovation of the restaurant. The old site was once a segregated club. Anita Baker razed the building, gutting the historical fixtures and rebuilding from scratch. "Now," said William, "it is an African-American establishment." William noticed that he was the only white patron in the restaurant. He felt excluded by the cheerful banter between the African-American wait staff and their customers of color. His eggs were cold but he didn't want to complain. What would they think? He was the only white guy in the room. He didn't want to be a complaining white person. If he were in a white neighborhood (like the one where he grew up), would he then have sent them back? William tells me that his heart sank when the waitress passed him by, only to stop at the adjoining table of black customers to ask if there was anything she could do for *them*. "Were their eggs hot?", she asked. "I hoped I wouldn't have to mention this to you," said William, "but then when I got here it was all I could think about."

Let's examine what makes this the more complicated transaction. The clinical themes arguably are the same. William feels his familiar sense of estrangement, again conveying his feeling that he is not really entitled to his anger. He readily connects the scene with the waitress to his transference feeling that other people (i.e. my other patients, perhaps my black patients) get better treatment than he does. But William recognizes that this is an idea with a long history in William's life. "I hate the idea of someone else being important to you," he says, "I want more attention. It's the feeling that I had with my mom, that I always wanted more than what she wanted to give."

At the same time, as "the only white guy in the room", in both the restaurant and also in his analytic hour, William experienced his hurt in racial terms. William barely expects me to sustain interest in his everyday complaints; as "a complaining white person" he seems to feel that his cause would be completely lost.

As I listened to William, my own experience was equally complicated. I, like William, also understood that his more open participation in his analysis signaled genuine courage given his ready gravitation to self-protectively inhibit himself and his communications. All the same, I couldn't help but like the idea of Anita Baker demolishing that old restaurant and with it, a long-time standard of segregation. I became distracted during the session and my thoughts drifted to a news story about the Ku Klux Klan winning the right to "adopt a highway" in Missouri. Unable to stop the Klan, the Missouri State Legislature countered by renaming that same highway after Rosa Parks, effectively requiring the Klan to be in service to the mother of the modern civil rights movement.

Thus, even though my attention was focused on helping William to elaborate upon his experience, it was also the case that William's humiliation in the restaurant experienced in racial terms resonated for me with a moment of vicarious triumph. The racial talk "out there" when it is moved "in here" implicated us both in a cultural conversation. William and I were caught in the tension of being differently positioned, both together and apart. Although analyst and patient always have "inescapably and inherently diverging interests" (Slavin & Kriegman, 1998), I believe that the awareness of racial positioning may provoke tension of a different order given the historical social climate of the racial divide.

Dale Boesky (1990) has suggested that "if the analyst does not get emotionally involved in some way he [or she] had not intended, the analysis will not proceed to a successful conclusion" (Boesky, 1990, p. 572). Owen Renik (1993, 1996) has argued that enactments—unplanned relational engagements—are among the most basic forms of clinical relating. He advocates that psychoanalysts develop principles of technique that acknowledge that the analyst cannot know fully how he or she is participating in the exchange. For Renik, this means that clinical understanding is always retrospective, rather than predictive. Effective psychotherapy involves making these enactments subjects of reflection.

Elsewhere I have asked what happens when the enactment under question is a racial enactment (Leary, 2000). Does the same ethic of open exploration prevail? What facilitates or impedes our ability to work with the racialized subjectivity of the analyst and the patient? In a recent paper, Holmes (1999) writes that race and countertransference magnify each other's effects and can interfere with the therapist's capacity to be resourceful. I am in agreement with Holmes. In my own work, I have found it helpful to think of these experiences as involving "racial enactments". By racial enactment, I mean to designate those interactive sequences that embody the actualization in the clinical situation of cultural attitudes towards race and racial difference.

The following examples, drawn from the analytic literature, illustrate some of the forms a racial enactment may take. In her paper "Race and Transference," Kris Yi (1999) describes the case of C, a white male graduate student, presenting for psychotherapy at a university clinic. Assigned to an Asian female therapist, C reacted powerfully to his therapist's race. He told her that he experienced her accented English and "small voice" as unassailable signs of her inadequacy. He went on to say that in his experience Asian women were a "sexual fetish" for white men. The patient's sexist and racist comments, writes Yi, so horrified the therapist that the only thing she could think to ask was how the patient could have such judgments when he had very little knowledge of her. Although the patient went on to set his reactions in context—he had been abandoned by an Asian girlfriend—C and his therapist were not able to establish a working relationship with one another and the patient asked to be transferred to a white male therapist.

Neil Altman (2000) also describes a racial enactment in his paper "Black and White Thinking". Altman's African-American patient, Mr A regularly bounced the cheques for his treatment fees. Altman consistently pursued the dynamics behind Mr A's refusal to pay his bills. Mr A promised to make amends, resumed payments for a short while, only to bounce cheques again. In the process, Altman learned that Mr A had grown up in poverty in an inner city neighborhood in which Altman had once worked. In foster care for two years as a youngster because his parents couldn't handle his aggressive behavior, Mr A then turned his life around. He excelled academically and eventually graduated from the elite schools he attended on scholarship. Just before beginning treatment, Mr A had resentfully repaid money his father had loaned him at the request of his father's new wife. Despite what Altman and Mr A understood together, the bounced cheques continued.

Altman forthrightly examines his ensuing thoughts and feelings:

> Even before the first check had bounced, I had the marginal thought that Mr A would not pay me. I cannot be certain of all the sources of this thought, but I believe my thinking went like this: I can't believe this man who fought his way up from poverty and who still struggles to make ends meet, is going to pay substantial sums of money to a privileged person like me. At a somewhat deeper level was a racially prejudiced thought: I thought of him as more likely to stiff me because he was black. Feeding this thought were, I think, classism and stereotypes involving black people, irresponsibility and criminality. A complementary anti-Jewish stereotype was activated as well. I began to feel like the stereotypical greedy Jew, like the Jewish landlord feeding off the poverty-stricken residents of the ghetto. In the face of my sense of shame about all of these feelings, it was difficult to confront Mr A. about the bounced checks. [Altman, 2000, p. 594]

Despite Altman's efforts to show Mr A how the patient was repeating key parts of his lived relationship with his parents (Mr A felt he was owed something from his father for having abandoned him to foster care), Mr A left his therapy owing Altman a considerable amount of money. In my view the enactment continued as Altman persisted in sending Mr A bills for eight months, in the absence of any further communication with Mr A. In his case report, Altman seems to emphasize his continuing surprise that Mr A did not pay him even after a small claims judgment was rendered against him.

How might we understand these clinical vignettes? In her discussion of the case of C, Yi notes that the therapist's race evoked an intense negative reaction in the patient because race was organized in accord with fears that painful past experiences would be repeated (e.g. that his Asian therapist might abandon him as had his Asian girlfriend). For her part, with subsequent reflection, the therapist recognized that her uncharacteristic response to a patient's transference (in effect she basically said "how could you possibly think that?") stemmed from her own history of having been a victim of racist incidents. Quite understandably, she feared being victimized again as well.

Altman's emotionally frank consideration of his own attitudes allows him to locate his racial enactment in a projective–introjective matrix. I quote from Altman once again:

> My prejudicial image of Mr A served a defensive, projective function for me by protecting my preferred self-image as a responsible, solid citizen. Meanwhile, Mr A, I speculate, had internalized such denigrated images of himself as a black man. Within our interaction, this process was reinforced as Mr A presumably identified with my covertly racist image of him. He might have inferred that I had held such an image of him from, for example, my delay in confronting his bounced checks, as if I were bending over backwards to deny that I found his behavior irresponsible. [Altman, 2000, p. 597]

Similarly, in my experience with William, the patient and I easily became committed to a particular construction of racial experience. We became players, in this instance, in a silent movie involving the reversals of fortune and the story of symbolic black triumph over white aggression when I respond to his account of the restaurant with my fantasy of the freeway named for Rosa Parks. Importantly, *and only in retrospect*, did I realize that even as William experiences his rejection in racial terms, I coded his complaints as subtle provocations that I also registered racially. In remembering the news story about the freeway, I associated William's warded off aggression with the KKK, the most potent expression of white violence that exists for African-Americans. Again, my sense of this was that in doing so, William and I were now poised to discover how we were differently positioned, both together and apart.

In each instance, patient and therapist quickly became implicated in a cultural conversation. The ensuing strain illustrates what I believe is our collective susceptibility to the cultural milieu in which we live and of which the consulting room is a part. In this context, patient and analyst must also be understood to be racialized subjects.

Racial enactments are occasions, at least potentially, of clinical productivity to the extent that the analytic couple is able to tolerate and learn from their immersion in each other's psychology. At the same time, they are also moments of clinical exposure for both the analyst as well as for the patient. Cisz (1998) suggests that this may be so because of the distinctive nature of a racial enactment. She writes that although it is always possible that a therapist may unwittingly re-traumatize a patient in his or her care, the analyst can usually be assured that he or she played no role in the patient's original trauma. Racial enactments, however, offer no such reassurance. As Cisz notes, the institutional nature of racism and the differential privilege conferred on some members of a racial community means that the analyst, by virtue of her participation in the social world, may in fact, be complicit in some forms of oppression.

I believe it may also be fruitful to look outside of psychoanalysis to enhance our understanding of the racial enactments in the consulting room. In social psychology, studies of "implicit cognition", for example, demonstrate people's automatic preference for faces with Euro-American phenotypes over those with an African-American features, even on the part of those who profess non-racist values and ideologies (Greenwald & Banaji, 1995).

Claude Steele (1997, 1998) has used a model of stereotype threat–disidentification theory to examine group differences in performance on standardized tests by men and women and also by blacks and whites. Although black students begin school with test scores not too far behind those of their white counter-parts, a performance gap begins to appear in the opening years of elementary school. There are virtually no differences between boys and girls in performance on standardized tests until middle school when a trend towards males doing better steadily increases until high school. Steele suggests that the relevant dimension here is the relationship between the group to which the individual belongs and the domain under assessment—e.g. the stereotype that girls can't do maths; blacks aren't smart.

Steele argues that the test situation itself invokes a stereotype threat: a negative stereotype about a group to which one belongs becomes self-relevant. This causes what the social psychologists call "spotlight anxiety" (Cross, 1991, quoted in Steele, 1997) as the subject realizes that he or she could be judged or treated in terms of a racial stereotype ("if I don't do well on this test, they will think it's because I am black"). How threatening this recognition becomes depends on the person's identification with the stereotype-relevant domain. The effort to overcome stereotype threat by disproving the stereotype carries its own burdens as we all readily appreciate the way in which hyper-attention to any complex skill interferes with its smooth performance.

I believe that in the consulting room, racial enactments involve instances of stereotype activation. Patient, analyst or both are confronted with a self-image that threatens self-condemnation or judgment from the other. In addition to interfering with narcissistic equilibrium, the very effort to overcome the stereotype can disrupt the capacity for what Holmes (1999) elegantly describes as the therapist's ability to be resourceful. Instead, the analytic couple actualizes the very stereotyped transference or counter-transference each wished to ward off. This is how I understand how the therapist in Yi's case example becomes, in fact, unable to help C, just as the patient feared and why Altman remains locked into his enactment, unable to really believe that Mr A does not intend to pay him. For my part, I played right into William's transference hand by becoming, at least for the moment, as aggressively self-involved (with my fantasy of the Rosa Parks freeway) as William expects people to be and fears he will reveal himself to be if he is examined too closely.

Cushman (2000) suggests that effective engagement with racial process rests on therapists becoming skilled at "opening one's self up to difference" (p. 615). In Cushman's terms this requires analysts to be willing to:

[take] chances, to make mistakes and pick themselves up again, to face the worst of what pops into their minds and out of their mouths. That takes the capacity to grant one's self the freedom to be human, to recognize mistakes, to understand them, admit them, and continue in relationships with others. It takes the capacity to be open to others, to let them teach you something you don't know about them and something you don't know about you . . . [it requires] genuine conversation . . . [Cushman, 2000, p. 615]

Most broadly, this requires the analyst to recognize intersubjective content, to expect enactments and to treat them as relational opportunities. This is dependent on the capacity of patient and therapist (and supervisor) to establish conditions of safety such that they can tolerate their exposure to the other. In some contexts, the process may begin when the analyst faces up to racial contents that the analyst may not wish (or even really care to believe) are his or her own and accepts that these drive his or her behavior, including in the clinical situation. This offers at least the possibility of transforming stereotyped interchanges from moral and moralizing discourses into the pragmatics of living with and dealing with differences.

Conclusions

As we have seen, race remains a complicated business in our social and clinical worlds. Open talk about race invariably involves a turn to a conversation about racism, and threatens to expose the stake that any one of us may have in the defensive solutions racial reasoning provides.

Race and ethnicity are an important area for analytic inquiry. The analyst's working subjectivity regarding his or her racial assumptions must be subject to honest and compassionate scrutiny. This requires a willingness to bear a measure of discomfort in order to make it possible to learn with and from patients. If Winnicott was correct in suggesting that there is no such thing as a baby, then perhaps there is no such thing as a black or a white (without the other). Whenever patients talk about the Other, they are inevitably talking about themselves. And so are we.

References

Altman, N. (2000). Black and White thinking: A psychoanalyst reconsiders race. *Psychoanalytic Dialogues, 10*(4): 589–605.

Boesky, D. (1990). The psychoanalytic process and its components. *Psychoanalytic Quarterly, 59*: 550–584.

Cisz, J. (1998). Unpublished manuscript.

Cross, T. (1991). Cited in Steele, C. (1997). A threat in the air: How stereotypes shape intellectual identity and performance. *American Psychologist, 57*(6): 613–629.

Cushman, P. (2000). White guilt, political activity, and the analyst: Commentary on paper by Neil Altman. *Psychoanalytic Dialogues, 10*(4): 607–618.

Friedman, H. (2000). Unpublished paper—personal communication.

Greenwald, A., & Banaji, M. (1995). Implicit social cognition: Attitudes, self-esteem, and stereotypes. *Psychological Review, 102*(1): 4–27.

Holmes, D. (1999). Race and countertransference: Two "blind spots" in psychoanalytic perception. *Journal of Applied Psychoanalytic Studies, 1*(4): 319–332.

Jones, E. (1987). Psychotherapy and counselling with Black clients. In: P. Pederson (Ed.) (1987). *Handbook of cross-cultural counseling and therapy,* pp. 173–179. Westport, CT: Greenwood Press.

Lelyveld, J. (Ed.) (2001). *How Race is Lived in America: Pulling Together, Pulling Apart* by Correspondents of *The New York Times.* New York: Henry Holt.

Leary, K. (1995). Interpreting in the dark: Race and ethnicity in psychoanalytic psychotherapy. *Psychoanalytic Psychology, 12*: 127–140.

Leary, K. (1997). Race, self-disclosure and "forbidden talk": Race and ethnicity in contemporary clinical practice. *Psychoanalytic Quarterly, 66*(2): 163–189.

Leary, K. (2000). Racial enactments in dynamic treatment. *Psychoanalytic Dialogues, 10*(4): 639–653.

Renik, O. (1993). Analytic interaction: Conceptualizing technique in the light of the analyst's irreducible subjectivity. *Psychoanalytic Quarterly, 62*: 553–571.

Renik, O. (1996). The perils of neutrality. *Psychoanalytic Quarterly, 65*: 495–517.

Slavin, M., Renik, O., & Kriegman, D. (1998). Why the analyst needs to change toward a theory of conflict, negotiation, and mutual influence in the therapeutic process: Reply to commentary. *Psychoanalytic Dialogues, 8*(2): 293–296.

Steele, C. (1997). A threat in the air: How stereotypes shape intellectual identity and performance. *American Psychologist, 57*(6): 613–629.

Steele, C. M., & Aronson, J. (1998). Stereotype threat and the test performance of academically successful African Americans. In: C. Jencks &
M. Phillips (Ed.), *The Black–White test score gap: An introduction*, pp. 401–
427. Washington, DC: Brookings Institution.

Yi, K. (1988). Transference and race: An intersubjective conceptualization.
Psychoanalytic Psychology, 15(2): 245–261.

Response to Kimberlyn Leary's paper

Kate White

Thank you Kim for a rich and interesting paper that has helped me, and I hope you as the audience listening to Kim's presentation, to engage more deeply with questions that are both challenging and difficult to reflect on because they take us to places where power has been brutally exploited and where these differences have such a traumatic history. Our own personal stories are also activated in this discussion as was mine and thus so often we can become frozen, paralysed and drenched with shame and avoid the encounter. In my case I bring a history of growing up in South Africa in the early years of my life and then coming to the UK at secondary school age. The resonances of the conference theme are both deeply personal and also political as I face my own racialized thinking and behaviour and try to stay open in the conversation without "running for cover" (Straker, 2004a). I remember vividly as a child as well as now, when owning my South African roots and seeing the questioning look on peoples' faces (which I read as "well which side were you on?"), wanting to add very quickly—"and of course we had to leave because of the apartheid politics"—full of fear that I would be seen as a racist like the Nationalist Party Afrikaners. But also perhaps feeling satisfied that I was from a good "liberal thinking—anti apartheid family".

I have particularly appreciated Kim's opening to her paper which situates the writing of it in historical terms. She reminds us that what we are thinking and feeling and therefore reflecting upon today emerges from a particular context, immersed as she was as she wrote it then and as we all are listening to her now, in the continuing legacy of September 11th 2001. She cites the shock of white Americans as they became aware of the fact that they were and are being targeted because they are a member of a group. Gone was the security of being safe as an individual that many had grown up with. For many other Americans, immigrants and others, such an awareness has long been "a self-conscious fact" lived with every day. This is something so true of our situation here in the UK too, a fact Cascia Davis has reminded us of in her paper this morning.

I am reminded of my growing up in South Africa where as a privileged white girl I was made aware only gradually of the horror of the apartheid laws by which people were segregated from each other. I was a safe white individual. It was later, on my return to my home town as an adult that the shock of seeing the poverty of the township reached me anew. It was seeing the brutality as it was floodlit at night—huge arc lights piercing into fragile, makeshift corrugated tin "shacks" and I remembered the accounts of the difficulty people described in sleeping in such floodlit conditions with the sound of South African Army armoured vehicles circling the streets.

> ... the frightening awareness that one could be targeted simply because one is a member of a group. [Leary, 2006, p. 75]

Kim reminds us of how this fear has **always** been a part of many people's lives. As Farhad has described, the question is *which shape* are we highlighting at this particular point in history and how are these differences being used and manipulated to maintain particular power relationships? That is the question. So now it's the *Them* of people from Middle Eastern and South Asian and Muslim backgrounds that are being targeted for exclusion. I would agree with the quotation Kim cites from Kevin Pough, an African American ... *When all this goes all the way, when we put all the terrorists away, are we going to go back to the way we were before?*

How is race lived in psychotherapy?

Keeping the wider context in our minds—Kim's question to us is—
"so how is race lived in psychotherapy?". She identifies a gap that we
have here in the UK too, both in the literature, in our training and in
clinical practice. How are we influencing the provision and practice
of mental health care which is sensitive to the needs of people who
are already alienated and on the economic margins of our society?
We have examples like NAFSIYAT, The Women's Therapy Centre,
Immigrant Counselling and Psychotherapy, The Medical Foundation for the Care of Victims of Torture, The Separation and Reunion
Forum and others, all of whom have pioneered therapeutic services
for those on the edge. But what about training and supervision and
support in the hard pressed NHS framework? Here at CAPP we have
been developing a low cost psychotherapy service, The Blues Project,
offering access to a long term attachment relationship in which to
provide the possibility of recovery from disrupted early attachments.
We are looking at ways to share our experience where we may be
able to influence mental health care provision in other arenas.

Kim poses a very challenging question in her paper—how are we
to define new sites for psychologically relevant and emotionally
meaningful understandings of race? She suggests that we need to
explore and extend contemporary analytic concepts such as *enactment* and clinical *intersubjectivity* as well as exploring the contribution
from multicultural and research perspectives from other disciplines.
She offers us a clinical vignette of her own to illustrate this.

The clinical processes described by Kim are in sharp contrast to
more traditional and reactionary ways of relating to race in a therapeutic setting—in which race "matters" only as it enables access to
"psychoanalytic matters". For example, a person of mixed heritage
with whom I worked would anticipate my understanding of her
difficulties and "complaints about her experience at her college" as
typical of her, like so many black people walking around with a
"chip on the shoulder". Rather than recognizing that she had genuine cause for feeling hurt and marginalized by her tutors who had a
racist stereotyping of her as not being clever, hard working or cap-
able, she thought I'd see this as the result of early attachment trauma
skewing her perceptions rather than a reality of racist stereotyping
and invisibility.

So to Kim's account of her work with William. What I found so moving was the delicate and yet straightforward way she responded to his struggle to find a voice of protest at their separation. How she brought her absence into focus and understood his use of the image of the boat without its "black keel" as his way to organise their relational experience, acknowledging that she had left him beached. Race becoming, as Kim says, "a therapeutically available surface . . . to convey transference hopes and dreads" (Leary, 2006, p. 79).

I particularly appreciated Kim's analysis of the dangers of seeing reference to race (the patient's or analyst's) as merely the signifiers of deeper psychoanalytic meanings rather than a reference to the person's identity within the wider social context. For example, with my client I have already spoken about—she had very low self esteem and we had to work consistently on the erosion of her confidence by the internalized racism she had grown up with, a view of herself painfully confirmed on a daily basis by her continuing experience of racism on the course she was taking. Another strand was exploring its echoes with repeated early attachment difficulties where she struggled to be attuned to and valued by caregivers.

Kim draws our attention to the fact that we are engaged in a two person relationship—so what about the analyst's subjectivity, participation and contribution to the encounter? She emphasises the need for us to be open to honest and compassionate scrutiny. Here Kim takes us to the heart of the relational approach and demonstrates to us what she is talking about—her capacity both to reflect on her own thoughts and feelings and to use them in her understanding of the encounter with William. This takes courage. Access to her thoughts and feelings brings a whole new dimension—the racial talk "out there" moved into the room and she described both of them being caught in the tension of being differently positioned, both together and apart in relation to the "racial divide". The challenge here is in how we risk talking about that experience and keep the space open, rather than collapsing it into the comfort of finding our similarities.

Here I am reminded of a thought provoking set of papers by Gillian Straker (2004a, 2004b) and Melanie Suchet (2004a, 2004b), who explore the impact of their South African experience on their ability, in Muriel Dimen's words, to "consider the painfulness of political inequality, amidst therapeutic intimacy" (Dimen, 2000: 569).

In developing her concept of a *racial enactment* Kim illustrates this in sharing with us her internal thoughts and imaginings as she listens to William's description of being in the restaurant where he fears being seen as the complaining white man. She finds herself imagining her pleasure at being in the previously segregated restaurant now owned and filled with the glorious sound of a black woman jazz singer, and in contemplating the tables now being turned on the white racists of the KKK who have to support the renamed Rosa Parks highway celebrating the black liberation struggle. I wondered too about the gendered nature of these feelings of vicarious triumph. What is so revealing is how Kim is open to her reverie and uses it to help her find a more nuanced understanding of William's own hidden emotions

> by becoming, at least for the moment, as aggressively self-involved (with my fantasy of the Rosa Parks freeway) as William expects people to be (and fears he will reveal himself to be as well if he is examined too closely. [Leary, 2006, p. 86]

These are relational events characterized by strong emotions being stirred up in both analyst and analysand and as it is in this retrospective process of reflection that their meaning can be unravelled. An opportunity emerges for mutual transformation.

In the account by Neil Altman (2004), of the way he became caught up in the enactment of bounced cheques and then pursuing his patient for his unpaid fee, sadly a process of reflection was not possible. Altman in his work in this area talks of white liberal racism and he identifies a process of idealization, guilt and shame that immobilises us from truly intersubjective relating. Our benevolence towards the "other" forces the other person into a role of "being grateful" and may ultimately be a way of diffusing anger. Altman describes his fear of being seen as greedy, white and Jewish.

Kim eloquently states that:

> Racial enactments involve instances of stereotype activation. Patient, analyst or both are confronted with a self-image that threatens self-condemnation or judgment from the other. In addition to interfering with narcissistic equilibrium, the very effort to overcome the stereotype can disrupt the capacity for what Holmes (1999) elegantly

describes as the therapist's ability to be resourceful. Instead, the analytic couple actualizes the very stereotyped transference or countertransference each wished to ward off. [Leary, 2006, p. 86]

How fearful might we be that our countertransference may be coded in racialized terms? Stopping us in our tracks . . . Shutting down the exploration . . .

The implications of Kim's work for the education and training of psychotherapists are great. This is an area where we have a great deal of work to do. We have much to learn in our roles as teachers and supervisors. We need to take into account the dynamics of racial enactments both between supervisor and supervisee and between the supervisee and her clients, finding ways of enabling our students and ourselves to remain open to our emotional engagement with our clients.

I would now like to conclude by reminding you of Kim's own closing remarks:

Race and ethnicity are an important area for analytic inquiry. The analyst's working subjectivity regarding his or her racial assumptions must be subject to honest and compassionate scrutiny. This requires a willingness to bear a measure of discomfort in order to make it possible to learn with and from patients. [Leary, 2006, p. 87]

It seems to me that we are above all involved in a process of trying to recognise the impact of racism and stay with the struggle and the pain.

I leave you with this poem by Jackie Kay, a woman of mixed heritage who grew up in Glasgow

In my country

Walking down by the waters
down where an honest river
shakes hands with the sea,
a woman passed round me
in a slow watchful circle,
as if I were a superstition;

or the worst dregs of her imagination,
so when she finally spoke
her words spliced into bars
of an old wheel. A segment of air.

Where do you come from?

"Here," I said, "Here. These parts."

Jackie Kay, 1993, *Other Lovers*

References

Altman, N. (2004). Whiteness uncovered: commentary on papers by Melanie Suchet and Gillian Straker. *Psychoanalytic Dialogues, 14*: 439–446.

Altman, N. (2000). Black and White thinking: A psychoanalyst reconsiders race. *Psychoanalytic Dialogues, 10*: 589–605.

Dimen, M. (2000). Introduction to Symposium on Race. *Psychoanalytic Dialogues, 10*: 569–578.

Holmes, D. (1999). Race and countertransference: Two "blind spots" in psychoanalytic perception. *Journal of Applied Psychoanalytic Studies. 1*: 319–332.

Kay, J. (1993). In My Country. In: *Other Lovers*. Tarset: Bloodaxe.

Leary, K. (2006). How race is lived in the consulting room. In: K. White (Ed.), *Unmasking Race, Culture and Attachment in the Psychoanalytic Space: What do we see? What do we think? What do we feel?* pp. 75–89. London: Karnac.

Straker, G. (2004a). Race for cover: Castrated whiteness, perverse consequences. *Psychoanalytic Dialogues, 14*: 405–422.

Straker, G. (2004b). A Look Beyond the Mirror—What He Saw and I Didn't. *Psychoanalytic Dialogues, 14*: 447–452.

Suchet, M. (2004a). A relational encounter with race. *Psychoanalytic Dialogues, 14*: 423–438.

Suchet, M. (2004b). Whiteness Revisited: Reply to Commentary. *Psychoanalytic Dialogues, 14*: 454–456.

Ainsworth, M. (1967). *Infancy in Uganda: Infant Care and the Growth of Love.* Baltimore: Johns Hopkins Press.

Altman, N. (1995). *The Analyst in the Inner City: Race, Class, and Culture Through a Psychoanalytic Lens.* New York: Analytic Press.

Altman, N. (2000). Black and White thinking: A psychoanalyst reconsiders race. *Psychoanalytic Dialogues, 10*: 589–606; also Reply to Commentaries. *Psychoanalytic Dialogues, 10*: 633–638.

Altman, N. (2004). Whiteness uncovered: commentary on papers by Melanie Suchet and Gillian Straker. *Psychoanalytic Dialogues, 14*: 439–446.

Arnold, E. (1975). *Out of Sight Not Out of Mind.* M.Phil Thesis, University of Sussex.

Arnold, E. (1997). Issues of reunification of migrant West Indian children in the United Kingdom. In: J. L. Roopnarine & J. Brown (Eds.), *Caribbean Families: Diversity among Ethnic Groups.* Greenwich, CT: Ablex.

Arnold E. (2001) The hidden price of immigration. *Educational Therapy and Therapeutic Teaching. The Journal of the Caspari Foundation, 10.*

Arnold, E. (2003). Intercultural counselling in a social services setting. In: A. Dupont-Joshua (Ed.) *Working Inter-Culturally in Counselling Settings.* Hove: Brunner-Routledge.

Benjamin, J. (1998). *Shadow of the Other.* London: Routledge.

Bhugra, D., & Bhui, K. (1998). The psychotherapy for ethnic minorities: Issues, context and practice. *British Journal of Psychotherapy, 14(3)*: 310–326.

Blackwell, D. (1993). Disruption and reconstitution of family and community systems following torture, organized violence and exile. In: J. Wilson & B. Raphael (Eds.), *International Handbook of Traumatic Stress Syndromes*. New York: Plenum Press.

Blackwell, D. (2005). *Counselling and Psychotherapy with Refugees*. London: Jessica Kingsley.

Blakemore, K., & Boneham, M. (1994). *Age, Race and Ethnicity. A Comparative Approach*. Milton Keynes: Open University Press.

Botticelli, S. (1997). Theorizing the social in psychoanalysis. A review of: N. Altman (1995). *The Analyst in the Inner City: Race, Class and Culture through a Psychoanalytic Lens*. Hillside, NJ: Analytic Press. *Psychoanalytic Dialogues, 7*: 535–545.

Bowlby, J. (1988). *A Secure Base*. London: Routledge.

Boyd-Franklin, N. (1989). Therapist use of self and value conflict with Black families. In *Black Families in Therapy: A Multi Systems Approach*. New York: Guilford Press.

Brown, D. (1992). *Transcultural Group Analysis—Use and Abuse of Cultural Difference: Analysts and Ethics in Group Analysis*. London: Sage.

Carolan, M. T., & Allen, K. R. (1999). Commitment and constraints to intimacy for African American couples at mid-life. *Journal of Family Issues, 20(1)*.

Cassidy, J., & Shaver, P. (Eds.) (1999). *Handbook of Attachment: Theory, Research, and Clinical Implications*. New York: Guilford Press.

Cohen, S. (2001). *States of Denial*. Cambridge: Polity.

Colin, V. L. (1996). Cultural Variations in Attachment Relationships. In: *Human Attachment*, pp. 145–166. New York: McGraw Hill.

Cushman, P. (2000). White guilt, political activity, and the analyst: Commentary on paper by Neil Altman. *Psychoanalytic Dialogues, 10*: 607–618.

Dalal, F. (1988). The racism of Jung. *Race and Class 19(3)*: 1–22. Republished as: Jung a racist. *British Journal of Psychotherapy 4(3)*: 263–279.

Dalal, F. (1993). Race and racism—an attempt to organise difference. *Group Analysis, 26*: 227–293.

Dalal, F. (1993). The meaning of boundaries and barriers in the development of cultural identity. In: W. Knauss and U. Keller (Eds.), *Ninth European Symposium in Group Analysis "Boundaries and Barriers"*. Heidelburg: Mattes Verlag.

Dalal, F. (1997). A transcultural perspective on psychodynamic psychotherapy. *Group Analysis, 30*: 203–215.

Dalal, F. (1997). The colour question in psychoanalysis. *Journal of Social Work Practice, 11*: 2.

Dalal, F. (1998). *Taking the Group Seriously: Towards a Post Foulkesian Group Analytic Theory*. London: Jessica Kingsley.

Dalal, F. (1999). The meaning of boundaries and barriers in the development of cultural identity and between cultures. *Psychodynamic Counselling, 5(2)*: 161–171.

Dalal, F. (2001). Insides and outsides: a review of psychoanalytic renderings of difference, racism and prejudice. *Psychoanalytic Studies, 3*: 43–46.

Dalal, F. (2002). *Race, Colour and the Processes of Racialization: New Perspectives from Group Analysis, Psychoaanalysis and Sociology*. Hove: Brunner-Routledge.

Dimen, M. (2000). Introduction to Symposium on Race. *Psychoanalytic Dialogues, 10*: 569–578.

Dimen, M., & Goldner, V. (Eds.) (2002). *Gender in Psychoanalytic Space—Between Clinic and Culture*. New York: Other Press.

Dwivedi, K. N. (Ed.) (2002). *Meeting the Needs of Ethnic Minority Children: A Handbook for Professionals*. London: Jessica Kingsley Publishers.

Dupont-Joshua, A. (1997). Working with Issues of Race. *Counselling*, November: 282–284.

Eleftheriadou Z. (1994). *Transcultural Counselling*. London: Central Publishing House.

Eleftheriadou, Z. (1997). Cultural differences in the therapeutic relationship. In: I. Horton, & V. Varma, *The Needs of Counsellors and Psychotherapists*. London: Sage.

Eleftheriadou, Z. (1999). Assessing the counselling needs of ethnic minorities in Britain. In: P. Laungani, & S. Palmer (Eds.) *Counselling in a Multicultural Society*. London: Sage.

Eleftheriadou, Z. (Ed.) (1999). Special issue on racial and cultural differences. *Psychodynamic Counselling, 5*: 2.

Eleftheriadou, Z. (2003). Cross-cultural Counselling Psychology. In: R. Woolfe, W. Dryden, & S. Strowbridge (Eds.), *Handbook of Counselling Psychology*. London: Sage.

Eng, D. L., & Han, S. (2000). A Dialogue on Racial Melancholia. *Psychoanalytic Dialogues, 10*: 667–700.

Eng, D. L., & Han, S. (2001). A Dialogue on Racial Melancholia. In: S. Fairfield, L. Layton., & C. Stack (Eds.), *Bringing the Plague: Toward a Postmodern Psychoanalysis*, pp. 233–267. New York: Other Press.

Fanon, F. (1967a). *The Wretched of the Earth*. Harmondsworth: Penguin.

Fanon, F. (1967b). *Black Skins and White Masks*. Harmondsworth: Penguin.

Feagin J. R., & Sikes, M. P. (1994). *Living With Racism: The Black Middle-Class Experience*. Boston: Beacon Press.

Fernando, S. (1995). *Mental Health in a Multi Ethnic Society*. London: Routledge.

Fernando, S. (1999). Race in the Construction of Dangerousness. 6th John Bowlby Memorial Lecture. Centre for Attachment-based Psychoanalytic Psychotherapy (CAPP).

Flax, J. (1998). *The American Dream in Black and White: The Clarence Thomas Hearings*. Ithaca, NY: Cornell University Press.

Fletchman Smith, B. (2000). *Mental Slavery: Psychoanalytic Studies of Caribbean People*. London: Rebus Press.

Frampton, P. (2004). *Golly in the Cupboard*. Manchester: Tamic Publications.

Frosh, S. (1989). Psychoanalysis and Racism. In: B. Richards (Ed.), *Crises of the Self: Further Essays on Psychoanalysis and Politics*, pp. 229–244. London: Free Association Books.

Gordon, P., & Klug, F. (1984). *Racism and Discrimination in Britain; A select bibliography*. London: The Runnymede Trust.

Gordon P. (1993). Souls in Armour: Thoughts on Psychoanalysis and Racism, *British Journal of Psychotherapy*, 10(1).

Gordon, P. (2004). Souls in Armour: Thoughts on Psychoanalysis and Racism. With some further thoughts by the author. *British Journal of Psychotherapy*, 21: 277–298.

Green, M. (1987). Women in the oppressor role: white racism. In: S. Ernst & M. MacGuire (Eds.), *Living with the Sphinx; Papers from the Women's Therapy Centre*, ch. 7. London: Womens Press.

Gump, J. (2000). A white therapist, an African American patient—shame in the therapeutic dyad: Commentary on paper by Neil Altman. *Psychoanalytic Dialogues*, 10: 619–632.

Harris, A. (2000). Haunted talk, healing action. Commentary on paper by Kimberlyn Leary. *Psychoanalytic Dialogues*, 10: 655–662.

Harwood, R. (1995). *Culture and Attachment: Perceptions of the Child in Context*. New York: Guilford Press.

Herman, J. (1992). *Trauma and Recovery*. New York: Basic Books.

Hollander, N. (1997). *Love in a Time of Hate—Liberation Psychology in Latin America*. New Brunswick: Rutgers University Press.

Hollander, N. (1998). Exile: Paradoxes of Loss and Creativity, 5th John Bowlby Memorial Lecture. *British Journal of Psychotherapy*, 2: 201–215.

Kareem J. and Littlewood R. (1992). *Intercultural Therapy: Themes, Interpretation and Practice*. Oxford: Blackwells.

Kovel, J. (1970). *White Racism: A Psychohistory*. New York: Pantheon Books.

Kovel, J. (2000). Reflections on *White Racism. Psychoanalytic Dialogues*, 10: 579–588.

Krause, I. (1998). *Therapy across Culture*. London: Sage.

Kraemer, S., & Roberts, J. (Eds.) (1996). *The Politics of Attachment; Towards a Secure Society*. London: Free Association Books.

Lago, C., & Thompson, J. (1996). *Race, Culture and Counselling*. Milton Keynes: Open University Press.

Leary, K. (1995). Interpreting in the dark: Race and ethnicity in psychoanalytic psychotherapy. *Psychoanalytic Psychology*, 12: 127–140.

Leary, K. (1997). Race, self disclosure and "forbidden talk": Race and ethnicity in contemporary clinical practice. *Psychoanalytic Quarterly*, 66: 163–189.

Leary, K. (1999). Passing, posing and "keeping it real". *Constellations*, 6: 85–96.

Leary, K. (2000). Race in Psychoanalytic Space. In: M. Dimen, & V. Goldner (Eds.), *Gender in Psychoanalytic Space—Between Clinic and Culture*, pp. 313–330. New York: Other Press.

Leary, K. (2000). Racial enactments in dynamic treatment. *Psychoanalytic Dialogues*, 10: 639–654.

Leary, K. (2000). Reply to Commentary. *Psychoanalytic Dialogues*, 10: 663–666.

Lesser, R. C. (2001). Discussion of A Dialogue on Racial Melancholia. In: S. Fairfield, L. Layton & C. Stack (Eds.), *Bringing the Plague: Toward a Postmodern Psychoanalysis*, pp. 269–278. New York: Other Press.

Levy, A. (2004). *Small Island*. London: Review.

Laub, D., & Auerhahn, N. (1989). Failed empathy: A central theme in the survivor's Holocaust experience. *Psychoanalytic Psychology*, 6: 377–400.

Littlewood R., & Lipsedge M. (1989). *Aliens and Alienists—Ethnic Minorities and Psychiatry*. London: Unwin Hyman.

Lousada, J. (1997). The hidden history of an idea: The difficulties of adopting anti-racism. In: E. Smith (Ed.), *Integrity and Change: Mental Health in the Market Place*. Routledge, London.

Malek, M., & Joughin, C. (2004). *Mental Health Services for Minority Ethnic Children and Adolescents*. London: Jessica Kingsley.

Marris, P. (1996). *The Politics of Uncertainty: Attachment in Private and Public Life*. London: Routledge.

Marris, P. (1996). The Management of Uncertainty. In: S. Kraemer, & J. Roberts (Eds.), *The Politics of Attachment; Towards a Secure Society*. London: Free Association Books.

Marsela, A. G. *et al.* (1996). *Ethnocultural aspects of Post Traumatic Stress Disorder. Issues, Research and Clinical Applications*. American Psychological Association.

Moodley, R. (2000). Counselling and psychotherapy in a multicultural context: some training issues, Parts 1 and 2. *Counselling*, April/May: 221–224.

Morgan, H. (1998). Between Fear and Blindness: The White Therapist and the Black Patient. *Journal of The British Association of Psychotherapy*, 3 (34).

Mistry, T., & Brown, A. (1997). *Race and Group Work*. London: Whiting and Birch.

Orbach, S. (1999) Fat is a . . . Issue. In: *The Impossibility of Sex*, pp. 94–125. Harmondsworth: Penguin.

Papadopoulos, R., & Hall, B., (Eds.), (1997). *Multiple Voices: Narrative in Systemic Family Psychotherapy*. London: Routledge.

Papadopoulos, R. (1999). Storied Community as Secure Base. A response to Nancy Hollander, Exile: Paradoxes of Loss and Creativity—6th John Bowlby Memorial Lecture. *British Journal of Psychotherapy*, 3: 322–332.

Papadopoulos, R. K. (2002). Refugees, home and trauma. In: R. K. Papadopoulos (Ed.), *Therapeutic Care for Refugees. No Place Like Home*. London: Karnac.

Papadopoulos, R. K. (2002). "But how can I help if I don't know?" Supervising Work With Refugee Families. In: D. Campbell & B. Mason (Eds.), *Perspectives on Supervision*. London: Karnac.

Papadopoulos, R. K. (2002). Destructiveness, atrocities and healing: epistemological and clinical reflections. In: C. Covington, P. Williams, J. Arundale, & J. Knox, *Terrorism and War. Unconscious Dynamics of Political Violence*. London: Karnac.

Papadopoulos, R. K. (2002). The other Other: When the exotic Other subjugates the familiar Other. *Journal of Analytical Psychology*, 47(2): 163–188.

Papadopoulos, R. K. (2005). Political Violence, Trauma and Mental Health Interventions. In: D. Kalmanowitz & B. Lloyd (Eds.), *With art. Without illusion. Art Therapy and Political Violence*. London: Brunner-Routledge.

Pellegrini, A. (2000). Normalizing Citizenship, Forgetting Difference. A Review Essay of J. Flax (1998). *The American Dream in Black and White: The Clarence Thomas Hearings*. Ithaca, NY: Cornell University Press, in *Psychoanalytic Dialogues*, 10: 619–632.

Perez-Foster, M., Moskowitz, M., & Javier, R. (Eds.) (1996). *Reaching Across the Boundaries of Culture and Class: Widening the Scope of Psychotherapy*. Northvale, NJ: Aronson.

Raftery, M., & O'Sullivan, E. (1999). *Suffer the Little Children; the inside of Ireland's industrial schools*. Dublin: New Island Books.

Richards, B. (1989). *Crises of the Self: Further Essays on Psychoanalysis and Politics*. London: Free Association Books.

Sabbadini, A. (1996). From wounded victim to scarred survivors. Psychotherapy with victims of torture. *British Journal of Psychotherapy*, 12: 513–531.

Straker, G. (2004). Race for cover: Castrated whiteness, perverse consequences. *Psychoanalytic Dialogues*, 14: 405–422.

Straker, G. (2004) A Look Beyond the Mirror—What He Saw and I Didn't. *Psychoanalytic Dialogues*, 14: 447–452.

Suchet, M. (2004). A relational encounter with race. *Psychoanalytic Dialogues*, 14: 423–438.

Suchet, M. (2004). Whiteness Revisited: Reply to Commentary. *Psychoanalytic Dialogues*, 14: 453–456.

Swartz, L. (1998). *Culture and Mental Health: A Southern African View*. Capetown: Oxford University Press.

Tang, N. and Gardner, J. (1999). Race, culture and psychotherapy; Transference to minority therapists. *Psychoanalytic Quarterly*, 1: 1–20.

Thomas, L. (1995). Psychotherapy in the context of race and culture: an intercultural therapeutic approach. In: S. Fernando (Ed.), *Mental Health in a Multi Ethnic Society*. London: Routledge.

Thomas, L. (1996). Multicultural aspects of attachment theory. In *Race Newsletter*, BAC 1996.

Thomas L. (1998). A review of the article by H. Morgan: Between fear and blindness: the white therapist and the black patient. *Journal of the British Association of Psychotherapy*, 3(34). In: *The Psychotherapist*, 11: 8. Autumn. London: UKCP.

Timimi, S. (1996). Race and colour in internal and external reality. *British Journal of Psychotherapy*, 13: 2.

Tomlinson, M. (1997). Pathways to attachment; strange situation and culture in the South African context. *Southern African Journal of Child and Adolescent Mental Health*, 9(2) 107–122.

van Ijzendoorn, M.,& Sagi, A. (1999). Cross cultural patterns of attachment: universal and contextual dimensions. In: J. Cassidy & P. Shaver (Eds.), *Handbook of Attachment Theory, Research and Clinical Implications*. New York: Guilford Press.

Ward, I. (1996). Race and Racism. Reply to Sami Timimi. *British Journal of Psychotherapy*, 13: 2.

Waters, E., & Valenzuela, M. (1999). Explaining disorganized attachment: clues from research on mild-to-moderately undernourished children in Chile. In: J. Solomon and C. George (Eds.), *Attachment Disorganization*. New York: Guilford Press.

White, K. (Ed.) (2006). *Unmasking Race, Culture and Attachment in the Psychoanalytic Space: What do we see? What do we think? What do we feel?* London: Karnac.

Zevalkink, J. *et al.* (1999). Attachment in the Indonesian caregiving context. *Social Development*, 8: 21–40.

Zulueta, F. de. (1993). *From Pain to Violence: The Traumatic Roots of Destructiveness*. London: Whurr.

Zulueta, F. de. (1993). The Dehumanization of the "Other". In: F. de Zulueta, *From Pain to Violence: The Traumatic Roots of Destructiveness*, pp. 225–247. London: Whurr.

INTRODUCTION TO THE CENTRE FOR ATTACHMENT-BASED PSYCHOANALYTIC PSYCHOTHERAPY

The Centre for Attachment-based Psychoanalytic Psychotherapy (CAPP) is an organization committed to the development of this particular approach to psychotherapy. It provides a four-year training for psychotherapists and a consultation and referral service.

Attachment-based psychoanalytic psychotherapy has developed on the basis of the growing understanding of the importance of attachment relationship to human growth and development throughout life. This approach to psychotherapy, developing from the relational tradition of psychoanalysis, draws upon psychoanalytic insights and the rapidly growing field of attachment theory.

Understanding psychotherapy within the context of attachment relationships leads to an approach to psychotherapy as a co-operative venture between therapist and client. The aim is to develop a sufficiently secure base to enable the exploration of loss and trauma in the course of development. The therapy is designed to create a safe space in which the client can reflect upon their lived experience, their experience of relationships in the present, and their experience of their relationship with the therapist.

Mourning is vital to the acknowledgement and understanding of the effects of abandonment, loss, abuse, whether emotional, sexual, or physical. The support of an authentic process of mourning forms a central part of the therapeutic work. This is crucial to the development of a sense of self, and the capacity to form and sustain intimate relationships. Both a strong sense of self and good attachment relationships are essential to managing stressful experiences.

The losses and traumas to be addressed in therapy are not confined to a private world or to early life. Groups and society as a whole shape attachment relationships formed by individuals. The experience of loss and abuse as a result of structures and pressures and everyday experiences concerning race, gender, sexuality, class, culture and disability, together with the complexity of the individual's response, can be worked with in a profound way through attachment-based psychoanalytic psychotherapy.

John Bowlby's original development of attachment theory was promoted primarily by his concern to ensure social recognition for the central importance of attachment and the experience of loss in early development. He was also concerned to strengthen the scientific foundations for psychoanalysis. Since his original work attachment theory has come to occupy a key position in this fast growing scientific field. Attachment theory provides a crucial link between psychoanalysis, developmental psychology, neurobiology and the behavioural sciences.

CAPP has drawn on a wide range of approaches including the British Object Relations tradition, American Relational Psychoanalysis, theories on the development of the self, and contemporary work on trauma and dissociation to provide a breadth and depth of insight into the structure and dynamics of the internal world. The common themes that run through them all are the importance of unconscious communication, of the transference and the countertransference, of containment and the acceptance of difference, and an emphasis on two person psychology.

The development of our theoretical base is a dynamic and continuing process. The Centre will continue to adapt and develop in the light of new research, contemporary developments and clinical experience.